COBOL

Kenneth P. Seidel

COBOL

© 1971 by
GOODYEAR PUBLISHING COMPANY, INC.

Library of Congress Catalog Card Number: 76-145890

ISBN: 0-87620-185-0

Y-1850-0

Current printing (last number):

10 9 8 7 6 5 4 3 2 1

Printed in the United States of America

COBOL

KENNETH P. SEIDEL

GOODYEAR PUBLISHING COMPANY, INC.

Pacific Palisades, California

CONTENTS

ACKNOWLEDGEMENT

The following information is reprinted from COBOL Edition 1965, published by the Conference on Data Systems Languages (CODASYL), and printed by the U.S. Government Printing Office:

Any organization interested in reproducing the COBOL report and specifications in whole or in part, using ideas taken from this report as the basis for an instruction manual or for any other purpose is free to do so. However, all such organizations are requested to reproduce this section as part of the introduction to the document. Those using a short passage, as in a book review, are requested to mention "COBOL" in acknowledgment of the source, but need not quote this entire section.

COBOL is an industry language and is not the property of any company or group of companies, or of any organization or group of organizations.

No warranty, expressed or implied, is made by any contributor or by the COBOL Committee as to the accuracy and functioning of the programming system and language. Moreover, no responsibility is assumed by any contributor, or by the committee, in connection therewith.

Procedures have been established for the maintenance of COBOL. Inquiries concerning the procedures for proposing changes should be directed to the Executive Committee of the Conference on Data Systems Languages.

The authors and copyright holders of the copyrighted material used herein

FLOW-MATIC (trademark of Sperry Rand Corporation), Programming for the Univac (R)I and II, Data Automation Systems copyrighted 1958, 1959, by Sperry Rand Corporation; IBM Commercial Translator Form No. F28-8013, copyrighted 1959 by IBM; FACT, DSI 27A52602760, copyrighted 1960 by Minneapolis-Honeywell

have specifically authorized the use of this material in whole or in part, in the COBOL specifications. Such authorization extends to the reproduction and use of COBOL specifications in programming manuals or similar publications.

INTRODUCTION

This book is designed to provide the beginning COBOL programmer with a sound understanding of the COBOL language and programming techniques. In addition, I have taken care to do more than merely expostulate the official descriptions of individual COBOL language components by showing how to use them together; warning of pitfalls; and suggesting good practices in program preparation, coding, and checkout. Finally, through inclusion of many illustrations and examples, theory is amply backed up with practical demonstrations of realistic COBOL work.

The primary orientation of this book centers about third-generation computer systems—specifically the IBM System 360, RCA Spectra 70, and XDS Sigma families. These systems are at times contrasted with the Univac 1108 COBOL, used here as one example of COBOL on machines whose roots antedate the third generation.

I wish to thank Information Storage Systems, Inc., Cupertino, California, for permission to use their IBM System 360/30 in preparing sample program listings; and Mr. William C. Mallonee of Xerox Data Systems, El Segundo, California, for his co-operation in preparing the Sigma 7 run included here as Appendix E.

COBOL

1

WHAT IS COBOL?

1.1 History of COBOL

In the late 1950's, Codasyl (Committee on Data Systems Languages) was formed under the sponsorship of the United States Department of Defense. The committee was staffed with computer experts from a representative sampling of major industrial firms and computer manufacturing companies.

The charter of Codasyl specified that the committee was to develop a high-level computer language oriented toward business data processing that would be independent of the then current and future computer design characteristics. Programs written in such a language would be operable on a wide variety of different computers. Thus, when the staff of a computer installation was ready to upgrade its equipment by acquiring a faster and more modern computer, the necessity to rewrite programs developed over a long period of time would be minimized, if not entirely eliminated. This concept had recently been implemented in the engineering/scientific computing community, with the introduction by IBM of the Fortran language on its Model 704 computer.

Additional objectives of the Codasyl effort included a desire to make the new language clear and straightforward, so that its programs could be more easily understood than those written in machine-language or symbolic assembly-language coding.

Another benefit the committee anticipated was that programmers would be able to produce workable ("checked out") programs in less time than was normally possible when they worked in the tricky machine-oriented languages. This provided most of the economic justification for industry's participation in Codasyl's deliberations.

In 1960, Codasyl published the first description of COBOL–the *C*ommon *B*usiness-*O*riented *L*anguage.

In the beginning, it was popular to criticize the new language. Indeed, the charges of "it's too verbose" or "it's full of redundancies" were somewhat justified. And early attempts to equip various computers with the sophisticated translator programs to make COBOL operable were frequently unsatisfactory.

With the passage of time and by learning from mistakes in implementing the early COBOL translators, "software" experts eventually mastered the problems of making the COBOL language into a reality. During the same time, new developments in the techniques of producing computer hardware lowered the costs of electronic data processing, so that more and more businesses began to look to the computer to perform the essential information-handling tasks of everyday business.

Thus, by the middle of the 1960's, more and more computers were being used to do the type of work for which COBOL had been designed. And the need for ever-increasing amounts of programming made it imperative that a rapid means of program writing be made available to the industry. All these trends came together in the COBOL boom of the 1960's. Now it is widely recognized that for several years the predominant computer language has been COBOL.

1.2 Source and Object Programs

Programs written in symbolic computer language are called *source programs*. Cards keypunched from a programmer's coding sheets are a *source program deck*.

The source program is given as input to a special computer program called a *compiler*. The compiler program performs the complex task of translating the program statements (which were expressed by the programmer in COBOL) into a machine-language program understandable by the computer. The program produced by the compiler from a source program input is termed an *object program*. We say that the compiler has "compiled" the object program.

1.3 COBOL Program Structure

The COBOL programmer writes his COBOL statements on a coding form, or program sheet, such as the one shown in Figure 1-1. In so doing, the programmer must adhere carefully to the rules of the COBOL language in order to avoid a faulty compilation.

Every COBOL program must be divided into four divisions: Identification, Environment, Data, and Procedure. The divisions must appear in that order.

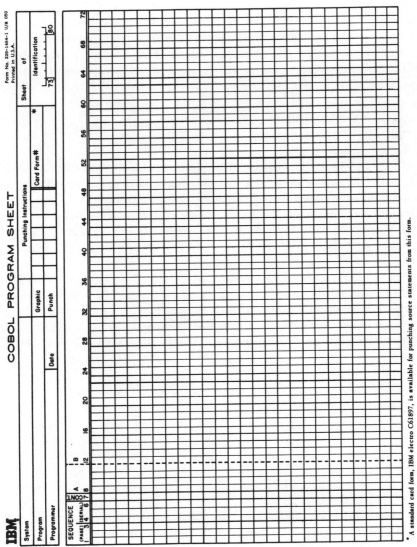

Figure 1-1 COBOL program sheet.

3

In general, each division is subdivided into sections; sections are subdivided into paragraphs; and paragraphs are composed of entries that consist of multiple clauses or statements. Thus, a COBOL source program has a hierarchical structure.

When writing COBOL programs, the user follows the predefined structure and wording of the particular program part (clause or sentence) that is required. A stylized notational form is employed in presenting the rules that govern COBOL statements. For example, one form of the ADD statement can be defined as:

$$\underline{\text{ADD}} \quad \begin{Bmatrix} \text{numeric-literal} \\ \text{data-name} \end{Bmatrix} \quad \cdots \quad \underline{\text{GIVING}} \text{ data-name} \quad [\underline{\text{ROUNDED}}]$$

The notation above means that the ADD statement must begin with the word ADD, spelled in upper-case letters. The line under ADD means that ADD is a reserved word which has a special meaning—it tells the compiler that you want to perform the addition of data values as one of the program steps. Because ADD is a reserved word, the user may not adopt ADD as the name of a data field, file, or procedure.

The braces ({ }) indicate that the user has a choice of two kinds of operands — either data-names or numeric literals (or both) must appear after the word ADD. The ellipsis marks (three dots) indicate that multiple appearances of the foregoing statement component may appear. The "square" brackets ([ ]) indicate that the enclosed statement components are optional.

By applying these rules, we can construct many different ADD statements:

ADD SALARY, OVERTIME GIVING GROSS-PAY ROUNDED.
ADD 1, X, Y GIVING XY1.
ADD FICA SDI INCOME-TAX GIVING DEDUCTIONS.

A stumbling block in learning COBOL is that it contains many reserved words. Unless the neophyte takes time to familiarize himself with these special words, he runs the risk of inadvertently selecting a reserved word in his choice of names for data, files, and procedures.

Therefore the beginning student of COBOL is well advised to study the reserved word list presented in Appendix A. Time spent in learning the reserved word list will be repaid in time saved in avoiding program errors which cause unnecessary delay in completing program development.

1.4 Punched Cards

The punched cards in which data is often recorded are a fairly commonplace item in modern society. It may be startling to most people to learn that the basic concept of representing data in punched cards dates as far back as the 1890 United States Census.

Herman Hollerith, an inventive scientist, devised the punched card concept to speed the massive census data-reduction task; he also invented hand-powered machines capable of "reading" the data from punched cards and tabulating the necessary summaries.

The punched card consists of a matrix having 80 columns and 12 rows. From the top of the card to the bottom, the rows are named 12, 11, 0, 1, 2, 3, 4, 5, 6, 7, 8 and 9, respectively. Columns are identified from left to right by the numerals 1 to 80, respectively.

To represent a digit, a single rectangular hole is punched in a given row. For example, the number 3280 might be represented as shown in Figure 1-2.

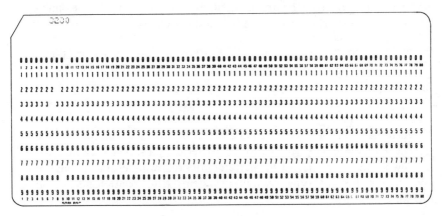

Figure 1-2   Punched card illustration.

Alphabetic data is represented in a systematic manner by combining two punches per column. The first third of the alphabet (the nine letters *A* through *I*) are represented by combining the digits 1 through 9 with a punch in the 12 row. The middle third of the alphabet (letters *J* through *R*) are represented by combining the digits 1 through 9 with a punch in the 11 row. The remaining portion of the alphabet (the *eight* letters *S* through *Z*) are represented by combining the digits 2 through 9 with a punch in the 0 (zero) row. Punches in rows 12, 11, and 0, when used as part of a multiple-punch character representation, are called "zone punches." (See Appendix B.)

Additional symbols which are required are represented by other multiple-punch combinations. Some of these combinations are different from one computer system to another. Appendix B illustrates the precise card punch conventions that are employed in three different systems: EBCDIC (used in the IBM System 360 family, among others); BCD (used in many computer systems antedating System 360); and a third system of yesteryear, the RCA 301.

1.5   Data Representation in Computer Memories

In general, there are two different methods of representing data characters in a computer, although only one method is employed in a given computer.

In one method, which is older and now on the wane, a character is represented by a pattern of six "bits," where a bit is a digit in the binary number system. The value of a bit is either 0 or 1. Thus, in a six bit pattern there are $2^6 = 64$ possible combinations of zeros and ones. Each character is represented internally by a unique bit pattern.

In what is today the predominant method of internal representation, each character is represented by a combination of eight bits. In this case, there are $2^8 = 256$ possible combinations of zeros and ones, so that a wide variety of different characters may be represented in the computer. For example, the lower-case alphabet can be represented in addition to the ordinary upper-case alphabetic characters.

The EBCDIC (Extended Binary Coded Decimal Interchange Code) convention is the most popular 8-bit character code. Another term describing an 8-bit character position is byte, pronounced "bite." EBCDIC is the built-in code employed in the IBM System 360, RCA Spectra 70, and XDS Sigma Series computer families.

When data characters are compared, comparison is on the basis of the equivalent of the binary (numeric) bit patterns. Thus, it is necessary to know that, owing to the choice of bit patterns, the following character relationships hold in the EBCDIC-type computer systems (this relationship is called a *collating sequence*):

```
blank  A  B  C  D  E  F  G  H  I
       J  K  L  M  N  O  P  Q  R
       S  T  U  V  W  X  Y  Z
       0  1  2  3  4  5  6  7  8  9
```

On the other hand, in systems employing six-bit character coding, the collating sequence may differ from that in EBCDIC. The usual form of the collating sequence is:

```
       0  1  2  3  4  5  6  7  8  9
       A  B  C  D  E  F  G  H  I
       J  K  L  M  N  O  P  Q  R
blank  S  T  U  V  W  X  Y  Z
```

The fact that collating sequences differ among many different computer systems means that sometimes *non-numeric* data comparisons may work differently on various computers. However, with respect to just the alphabetic characters, most collating sequences retain the usual alphabetic ordering scheme. Also, numeric comparisons are always performed in computers in such a way as to yield normal results in the arithmetic sense, and individual vagaries of computers constitute no impediment to conventional understanding.

Exercises

1. Describe, in your own words, the relationship between the source program, the COBOL compiler, and the object program.
2. Which of the following are reserved words in the COBOL language?

   DATA
   DATA-DIVISION
   PICTURE
   DEFINITION
   DIMENSION
   COMPUTE
   FORMAT
   READ
   WRITE
   PRINT
   PUNCH
   ZERO
   TEN
3. You are presented with a punched card on which the rows are identified, but there is no printed indication at the top of it. "Read" the columns and determine the message conveyed by the following card.

2

COBOL PROGRAM FUNDAMENTALS

2.1 Elements of a Program

A program is a proper combination of the following distinct elements:

words
numeric literals
non-numeric literals
pictures
level numbers and indicators
arithmetic operators
relational operators

Each of the above classes of elements has a precise definition. Elements are separated from one another by one or more blank spaces.

2.1-1 Words

In this book, we define a word to be a contiguous combination of up to 30 characters, using any of the following 37 different characters: letters A-Z, digits 0-9, and hyphen (or minus). A word must contain at least one alphabetic character. The hyphen may not be the first or last character of a word. From strict application of the above rules, we note that there may be no embedded blanks in a word. In general, the blank character (one or more) is used as a space

8

between words or other elements. We have just made an important point, which must be remembered in all COBOL programming. Punctuation may immediately follow a word in certain instances, such as at the end of a procedural sentence. In this case, one or more blanks must follow the punctuation.

Words are of two main types, reserved words, or user-supplied names. The following list illustrates such words:

INPUT-OUTPUT   reserved word

DATA   reserved word

ADD   reserved word

PICTURE   reserved word

SELECT   reserved word

A   user-supplied data-name

N10   user-supplied data-name

GRAND-TOTAL-LINE   user-supplied procedure name

OLD-MASTER-FILE   user-supplied file-name

2.1-2 Numeric Literals

Numeric literals consist of digits, an embedded decimal point (optional), and a leading minus sign (optional). A maximum of 18 numeric digits may appear in any literal.

Examples of numeric literals:

16

0001

−13

−44.63

2.1-3 Non-numeric Literals

A non-numeric literal is a string of not more than 120 characters enclosed in quotation marks.[1] Non-numeric literals consist of any characters representable in the computer, except for the quotation mark itself. This is the only source-language element that may contain a blank character.

---

[1] In many systems, the apostrophe or single quote is employed as the quotation mark. We will employ that convention throughout this book.

The following are examples of non-numeric literals:

'I AM A NON-NUMERIC LITERAL'
'JULY 4, 1776'
'*** CONTROL TOTALS DO NOT BALANCE ***'
'$'

If a non-numeric literal cannot fit entirely on one card of a source program, it may be continued onto the next card by using the following special continuation rule:

1. A hyphen is placed in column 7 of the continuation line.
2. A quotation mark is placed in Margin B preceding the continuation of the literal. (Margin B consists of card columns 12 to 72.)
3. All spaces at the end of the continued line and any spaces following the quotation mark in the continuation line and preceding the final quotation mark of the literal are considered part of the literal.

2.1-4 Pictures

A Picture is a special combination of characters used in describing data fields. Both the data length and a characterization of the kind of data (i.e., field content) are defined by the Picture, which follows the reserved word PICTURE in DATA-DIVISION entries. While it is premature at this point to delve deeply into the many rules that govern the formation of legal pictures, the following illustrations will serve as an introduction to these elements:

S9(5)V99 a numeric field, signed, five digits to left, two digits to the right of the assumed decimal point
X(47) a non-numeric string of 47 characters
ZZ,ZZZ.99CR a numeric edited field

2.1-5 Level Numbers and Indicators

Level numbers consist of one or two digits, and may be any of the following: 01-49, 77, 88. (In some compilers, level 66 is also available in connection with the RENAMES clause.) Level numbers, which convey the hierarchical nature of a data-record structure are treated fully in Chapter 4.

Level indicators for files (which are considered reserved words) are FD and SD. FD is explained in Chapter 4; SD is explained in Chapter 10.

2.1-6 Arithmetic Operators

There are five arithmetic operations in COBOL. For each of these, a particular symbology is employed:

+   addition
−   subtraction
*   multiplication
/   division
**   exponentiation

The exponentiation operator may only be written as two *consecutive* asterisks. In every case, an arithmetic operator must be both preceded and followed by at least one blank space.

A data-name is a programmer-supplied word designating a data field. Using data-names, numeric literals, and arithmetic operators, the COBOL programmer writes arithmetic expressions (calling for computations), such as the following:

A + B
FIT + SDI + FICA
ABSCISSA * 2
FN / FM − RATIO

2.1-7 Relational Operators

In the decision-making processes of a program, it is necessary to make comparisons between data-field values (or the results of an arithmetic expression). The relationships being tested may be equality, less than, or greater than. The three special characters =, <, or > may be employed to denote these relationships, respectively. Chapter 6 explains this subject in greater detail.

2.1-8 Figurative Constants

A figurative constant is a reserved word which symbolizes a pre-defined value:

ZERO   signifies a zero value (numeric)

SPACE   signifies the blank character (non-numeric)

HIGH-VALUE   signifies a non-numeric value represented by a binary 1 value in every bit position of a character.

LOW-VALUE   signifies a non-numeric value represented by a binary 0 value in every bit position of a character.

QUOTE   signifies the quotation mark character.

The plural form of spelling is permitted for each of these figurative constants.

Figurative constants may appear in many places where data-names or literals are permitted, notably in the VALUE clause, a MOVE statement, as an operand of a comparison in an IF statement, or in a DISPLAY statement; the discussion of these terms appears later in this text.

2.1-9   Format Notation

The format of a COBOL statement is described in this manual using the notational convention itemized below.

1. A COBOL reserved word, printed entirely in capital letters, is a word that is assigned specific meaning in the COBOL system. It must not be used in any context or position other than that shown in the format description.

2. One or more COBOL elements vertically stacked and enclosed in a set of square brackets [ ] indicate that this portion of the syntax is optional and may be included or omitted at the discretion of the programmer.

3. A pair of braces { } when used to enclose vertically stacked COBOL elements indicates that one, and only one, of the elements is required; the others are to be omitted.

4. The ellipsis . . . denotes a succession of operands or repeated COBOL elements that may be used in the same particular statement, even though the operands or elements are omitted in the text. An ellipsis is associated with the last complete element preceding it, e.g., if a group of operands and key words are enclosed within brackets and the right bracket is followed by the ellipsis, the group (and not merely the last operand) may be repeated in its entirety.

5. An underlined word is required unless the part of the format containing it is itself optional (enclosed in brackets). If a required word is omitted or incorrectly spelled, it causes an error in the interpretation of the program.

6. All optional COBOL words (not underlined) may be included or omitted at the option of the programmer. These words are used only for the sake of readability; misspelling, however, constitutes an error.

7. Lower case words represent information that is to be supplied by the programmer. The nature of the information required is indicated in each case. In most instances, the programmer is required to provide an appropriate data-name, procedure-name, literal, etc.

8. The period is. the only required punctuation. Other punctuation, where shown, is optional.

9. Special characters (such as the equal sign) are essential where shown, although they are not underlined in any example of statement syntax.

2.2 COBOL Coding Sheet

Referring to Figure 2-1, you may familiarize yourself with the use of the COBOL coding sheet. Columns 1-6, if used, must contain six-digit line numbers. Successive lines should have increasingly larger line numbers, so that the order of the source-program deck may be restored, should it become jumbled accidentally. Most compilers perform a sequence check, flagging any point in the program where an out-of-sequence condition exists. It is a good idea to assign successive line numbers in increments of 000010 or more so that there is room for insertions when the inevitable need for change arises.

Card columns 8-11 are called Margin A. All division headers, section names, and paragraph names begin in Margin A when they are being defined. The only other program elements that may appear in Margin A are level indicators (their position in Margin A is required) and level numbers (whose appearance in Margin A is optional).

Card columns 12-72, termed Margin B, are used for the remainder of all source-program parts. Card columns 73-80 are ignored by the compilers. Usually they are used for a common alphanumeric deck identification. Conceptually, one blank is assumed to be appended after column 72 on every line of a program sheet, except where a nonnumeric literal spans more than one line.

2.3 The Identification Division

Every COBOL program begins with an Identification Division. The division consists of commentary organized into paragraphs. Each paragraph-name is a reserved word. The paragraph-names are:

PROGRAM-ID
AUTHOR

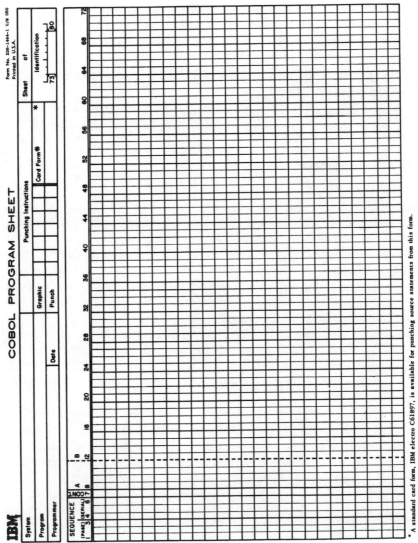

Figure 2-1.

14

INSTALLATION

DATE-WRITTEN

DATE-COMPILED

SECURITY

REMARKS

The Identification Division begins with the two reserved words IDENTIFICA-TION DIVISION. A period must immediately follow the second word. Of all the possible paragraphs in this division, only the PROGRAM-ID paragraph is required—and it must be the first one. The commentary in the paragraph provides the basis for assigning the name of the object program; the details of how this is done vary from compiler to compiler. In some IBM System 360 COBOL compilers, the PROGRAM-ID must be written as a non-numeric literal of no more than 8 characters long and is restricted to an exclusively alpha-numeric content.

All the remaining paragraphs in this section are optional, and there is complete freedom of choice as to their content. An example of an Identification Division for an IBM System 360 COBOL program is shown in Figure 2-2.

2.4 The Environment Division

The principal function of the Environment Division is to specify what external devices are associated with the data files to be processed by the program. Other functions specified in this division include:

1. describing the computer system's hardware components and features.
2. defining symbolic names for special hardware or software features, such as printer spacing-control functions or pocket selection on a card reader device.
3. special input-output techniques, such as mass-storage file processing software options.

In general, aspects of a program which are peculiar to a particular computer and its software system are concentrated in the Environment Division. The original intent of the Codasyl organization was to enable (to a maximum prac-tical extent) a program written for a computer of one manufacture to be manually adapted to a computer of a different manufacture by revising only the Environment Division. In actual practice, this is realistic only if the program's data descriptions are restricted to types of representation which are common to both computers.

IBM

COBOL PROGRAM SHEET

Form No. X28-1464-1 11/R 050
Printed in U.S.A.

System								Sheet	of
Program				Punching Instructions					
Programmer		Date	Graphic	Ø	O		Card Form #		*	Identification
			Punch	LETTER	DIGIT					SAMPLE

SEQUENCE		A	B					
(PAGE) 1 3	(SERIAL) 4 6	7 8	12	16	20	24	28	32	36	40	44	48
001010	IDENTIFICATION DIVISION.
001020	PROGRAM-ID. 'SAMPLE'.
001030	AUTHOR. NEØPHYTE PRØGRAMMER.
001040	REMARKS.
001050	ANYTHING YØU WANT TØ SAY HERE TØ
001060	DESCRIBE YØUR PRØGRAM ØBJECTIVIES.

* A standard card form, IBM electro C61897, is available for punching source statements from this form.

Figure 2-2.

16

The Environment Division consists of two sections, CONFIGURATION and INPUT-OUTPUT. The first is required; the second is optional, although it is usually also present, since few COBOL programs of any consequence exist which are not oriented toward processing one or more data files.

2.4-1 The Configuration Section

The Configuration Section has two required paragraphs and one optional paragraph. The general format of the Configuration Section is:

CONFIGURATION SECTION.
SOURCE-COMPUTER. computer-name.
OBJECT-COMPUTER. object-computer-entry.
[SPECIAL NAMES. special-names-entry...]

The computer-name is defined by each computer manufacturer. Some examples are tabulated below.

Computer	Source-computer-entry
IBM System 360	IBM-360.
RCA Spectra 70	[RCA-SPECTRA] [70-size] where size is a letter designating the memory size.
XDS Sigma	Any commentary text; e.g., XDS-SIGMA-7.
Univac 1108	UNIVAC-1108.

The OBJECT-COMPUTER paragraph has the general form:

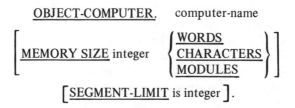

With the exception of the SEGMENT-LIMIT clause, both the SOURCE-COMPUTER and OBJECT-COMPUTER paragraphs are considered to be mere comments by most compilers. The segmentation feature is not found in all COBOL compilers. When it is implemented, the SEGMENT-LIMIT clause provides an essential item of information. However, this is an advanced topic that will not be considered in this introductory book.

The advanced user who requires a SPECIAL-NAMES paragraph must refer to the appropriate COBOL manual for determination of its form and meaning in any particular computer system.

2.4-2 The Input-Output Section

The Input-Output Section consists of two paragraphs. The first of these is the FILE-CONTROL paragraph; the second, which is optional, is the I-O-CONTROL paragraph. The general format of this section is:

$$
\left[
\begin{array}{l}
\underline{\text{INPUT-OUTPUT SECTION.}} \\[6pt]
\underline{\text{FILE-CONTROL.}} \quad \text{file-control-entry.} \ldots \\[6pt]
\left[\underline{\text{I-O-CONTROL.}} \quad \text{technique-entry.} \ldots \right]
\end{array}
\right]
$$

Each data file to be processed in a program is mentioned in a SELECT sentence, which constitutes a file-control-entry. Files are discussed in Chapter 5. A SELECT sentence may be defined by the following formal notation:

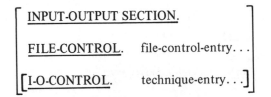

$$\underline{\text{SELECT}}\ \text{file-name}\ \underline{\text{ASSIGN}}\ \text{TO}\ \text{device-designation}$$

$$\left[\underline{\text{RESERVE}}\ \left\{\begin{array}{l}\underline{\text{NO}}\\ \text{integer}\end{array}\right\}\ \underline{\text{ALTERNATE}}\ \left[\begin{array}{l}\text{AREA}\\ \text{AREAS}\end{array}\right]\right]$$

$$\left[\underline{\text{ACCESS}}\ \text{MODE}\ \underline{\text{IS}}\ \left\{\begin{array}{l}\underline{\text{SEQUENTIAL}}\\ \underline{\text{RANDOM}}\end{array}\right\}\right]$$

A file-name is any unique user-supplied word Device-designations are specified by different computer manufacturing firms to conform to their particular hardware features and software nomenclature. Figure 2-3 illustrates what may be written in the ASSIGN clause for various computer systems.

The RESERVE clause gives the programmer the ability to control the number of buffers assigned to a file. A buffer is an area in memory into which (or from which) data is read (or written) during input-output operations. By stating RESERVE 1, the program will always have an alternate area available, so that there generally need be no waiting for input or output operations; by stating RESERVE NO, the program can be made more compact, at the possible sacrifice of increased execution time.

Sequential access implies serial (front-to-back) access to records so that record position is simply a function of time. The Access Mode Clause is normally specified only for mass-storage files (e.g., disk or drum devices). If ACCESS IS

Computer	Device Type	Device-designation
IBM System 360	Magnetic Tape	'SYSnnn' UTILITY 2400
	Card Reader	'SYSnnn' UNIT-RECORD 2540R
DOS (Disk Operating System)	Disk	'SYSnnn' DIRECT-ACCESS $\begin{Bmatrix} 2311 \\ 2314 \end{Bmatrix}$
	Line Printer	'SYSnnn' UNIT-RECORD 1403
		Where nnn are system unit numbers
Univac 1108	Magnetic Tape	UNISERVO file-letter
EXEC II Operating System	Card Reader	CARD-READER-EIGHTY
	Line Printer	PRINTER
		Where file-letter designates symbolically which tape drive is to be used, e.g., A or B, etc.
RCA Spectra 70	Magnetic Tape	'SYSnnn' UTILITY tape-model-number, e.g., M70-432, M70-442, M70-445
	Card Reader	'SYSnnn' UNIT-RECORD M70-237 or SYSIN
TDOS Operating System	Mass Storage	'SYSnnn' DIRECT-ACCESS $\begin{Bmatrix} M70\text{-}564 \\ M70\text{-}565 \end{Bmatrix}$
	Line Printer	'SYSnnn' UNIT-RECORD $\begin{Bmatrix} M70\text{-}242 \\ M70\text{-}243 \end{Bmatrix}$ or SYSOUT
XDS Sigma		Any implementor name from the following list: DISC, DRUM, CARD-READER, MAGNETIC-TAPE, PRINTER, CARD-PUNCH, TYPEWRITER.

Figure 2-3 Device assignment in typical COBOL compilers.

RANDOM is specified, the file is not accessed in the SEQUENTIAL (default) mode. On the other hand, RANDOM access implies that a specific record can be accessed (read or written); in this case, a special data field (key) is required to designate the specific record desired. Random access exploits special character-istics of mass-storage data-management systems, which permit storage and retrieval of records based on, for example, a set of unique part numbers in an inventory file or Social Security numbers in a personnel file. By the means of such "keys," direct reference may be made to the necessary records, without having to search through the entire file, which would be the normal method if the file were stored on magnetic tape instead of in mass storage.

For complete details on random-accessing techniques, consult the COBOL manual for the computer system in question.

The I-O-Control paragraph is available in different forms for various computer systems. This paragraph is considered an advanced and machine-dependent feature, and we need not say much about it now. One form of this paragraph, however, can be presented briefly at this time, as it is found in most compilers.

I-O-CONTROL.

RERUN [ON file-name-1] EVERY

$$\begin{Bmatrix} \text{integer } \underline{\text{RECORDS}} \\ \underline{\text{END}} \text{ OF } \underline{\text{REEL}} \end{Bmatrix} \text{ OF file-name-2.}$$

The RERUN entry specifies a quantitative criterion governing the issuance of checkpoint records. Checkpoint records constitute a complete capturing of the status of a program—both data and instructions, along with file-positioning parameters—so that, in the event of subsequent failure of the computer system, a lengthy computer run can be restarted at a mid-run point rather than from the beginning.

The RERUN entry specifies the device upon which the checkpoint records are placed. If ON file-name-1 is stated, the checkpoint records are transmitted to output file-name-1 in such a way that, when file-name-1 is processed in the normal way as an input data file, the checkpoint records are inconspicuous. In the absence of the ON file-name-1 specification, a standard checkpoint device is employed.

The criterion stipulating when checkpoint records are to be issued may be expressed in two ways:

1. integer RECORDS OF file-name-2. In this form, after processing the first n records of file-name-2, a checkpoint record is issued. After the next n records, another checkpoint record is issued. After the next n records, another checkpoint record is issued and so forth.

2. END-OF-REEL-OF file-name-2. In this case, when file-name-2 is a multi-reel file, the checkpoint issuance is triggered each time a full reel of tape is processed.

In some systems, it is also possible to specify a time period (integer CLOCK-UNITS) whose attainment triggers the issuance of checkpoint records. In the Univac 1108 COBOL, the RERUN entry must be preceded by the reserved word APPLY.

Exercises

1. Using the codes

    NL   for numeric literals
    QL   for non-numeric ("quoted") literals
    RW   for reserved words
    OP   for arithmetic operators
    RL   for relational operators
    AW   for arbitrary (user-supplied) words

    indicate the type of element that describes each of the following constructs.

    DATA
    1.67
    −3
    FD
    44
    A-44
    B500
    >
    =
    "RECORD"
    +

2. The maximum length of a word (reserved word or user-supplied name for files, data, or a procedure) is_____ characters.

3. The maximum length of a non-numeric literal is_____ characters, excluding the quotation marks.

4. In your own words, state the restrictions on use of Margin A (card columns 8-11), citing what program parts must, and what parts of a program must not, appear therein.

5. Study the programs in Appendixes C and D to make sure that you grasp the significance and meaning of the Environment Division.

6. What character separates successive words of a source program?

7. State the rules for constructing valid numeric literals.

3

DATA FILES

3.1 The File Concept

A file is a collection of related data (information) recorded in discrete records. Examples abound in everyday life: a business firm's personnel records constitute one kind of file; their accounts payable constitute another kind of file; their inventory and customer billing applications also employ appropriate files of data. The recording media for files may include such computer equipment as magnetic tape, punched cards, or magnetic disk packs or drums (collectively termed mass-storage devices). Printed data (reports) are also usually considered to be a file. There are three I-O modes in processing files: input, output, or combined input-output. Figure 3-1 relates these modes to the various device types.

Device Type	Permissible I-O Mode(s)
Card Reader	Input
Magnetic Tape	Either input or output
Mass Storage	Input or output or input-output
Line Printer	Output
Card Punch	Output

Figure 3-1 Relationship between devices and I-O modes.

22

3.2 The Record Concept

In simply structured files, every record has the same structure, but each record contains different data values that uniquely identify a distinct portion of data. In a personnel file, for example, each record corresponds to a particular employee. The "size" of the file, then, is determined by the number of records—in our example, by the number of employees. Of course, the size of the file also depends on the size of each individual record. For certain information devices, the size of the record is invariant. Such a device is the card reader, which reads a standard 80-column punched card. On the other hand, records on magnetic tape can be of essentially any length. The term *unit-record* refers to recording media whose record size is invariant: card readers, card punches, and line printers belong in this category.

3.3 Fields of Data

Each data record consists of a collection of fields. In a personnel file, each record might contain such fields as:

1. name of employee
2. Social Security number
3. address
4. birth date
5. hire date
6. department
7. hourly pay rate
8. year-to-date gross
9. year-to-date Federal income tax withheld
10. year-to-date F.I.C.A. deduction

For each of these fields, space is reserved to retain the appropriate data values exclusively. In general, data falls into two major categories—numeric and non-numeric—and can be of any length appropriate to the intent of the field in question. In most computers, there is more than one method of representing numeric data.

3.4 Multi-type Record Files

It is fairly common for files to contain records which do not all conform to a single structure. In this case, it must be possible to distinguish which type of record structure describes any given record so that the data may be dealt with by use of the proper set of field names. Therefore each of the different record structures must have some portion in common; the content of this common portion can be tested for different data values in order to establish the type of record currently available, and to permit the proper path of processing to be chosen. Let us consider a simple example. In creating a new employee's record in a personnel file, the data for the employee may be keypunched in a pair of cards, as illustrated in Figure 3-2.

The program which creates the new record must read data from two consecutive cards. One card must be a "type 1" card, identified by the presence of 1 in column 71. The other card must be a "type 2" card, identified by the presence of 2 in column 71. In order to make sure that these two cards go together, the program will check to see if the same Social Security number appears in both of the cards.

Once this is verified (and the data is in error if any of the verifications is not passed successfully[2]), processing can go on to develop fully the desired data record for the new ("updated") personnel file. The record that is developed from data taken from a good card pair may have any desired format, unconstrained by the fact that the data were originally in another format in certain columns of a pair of 80-column cards. Also, there may be fields in the output in addition to data existing in the input card pair. For example, the year-to-date gross field may be set to zero, since the new employee has not yet received any income from the company.

3.5 Blocked Files

The term *blocking* refers to a technique by which higher efficiency in the utilization of external storage devices may be obtained. Blocking cannot apply to unit-record files.

On magnetic tape or mass-storage devices, there is a certain irreducible minimum space required to separate successive records. In view of the high density at which data is recorded, it becomes very inefficient to record each record separately. For example, on typical 800 bpi tape,[3] all the information containable on one punched card occupies 0.1 (one-tenth) inch—followed by 0.6 to 0.75 inch of record separation space. In this case, less than one-eighth of the tape space actually contains usable information.

---

[2] We will return to expand on this point later. At this juncture, we can only warn that a program that lacks data validation in the case where the data are "fresh from the real world" is both foolish and dangerous.

[3] Bpi (bits/inch) measures the number of characters that may be recorded per inch of tape length.

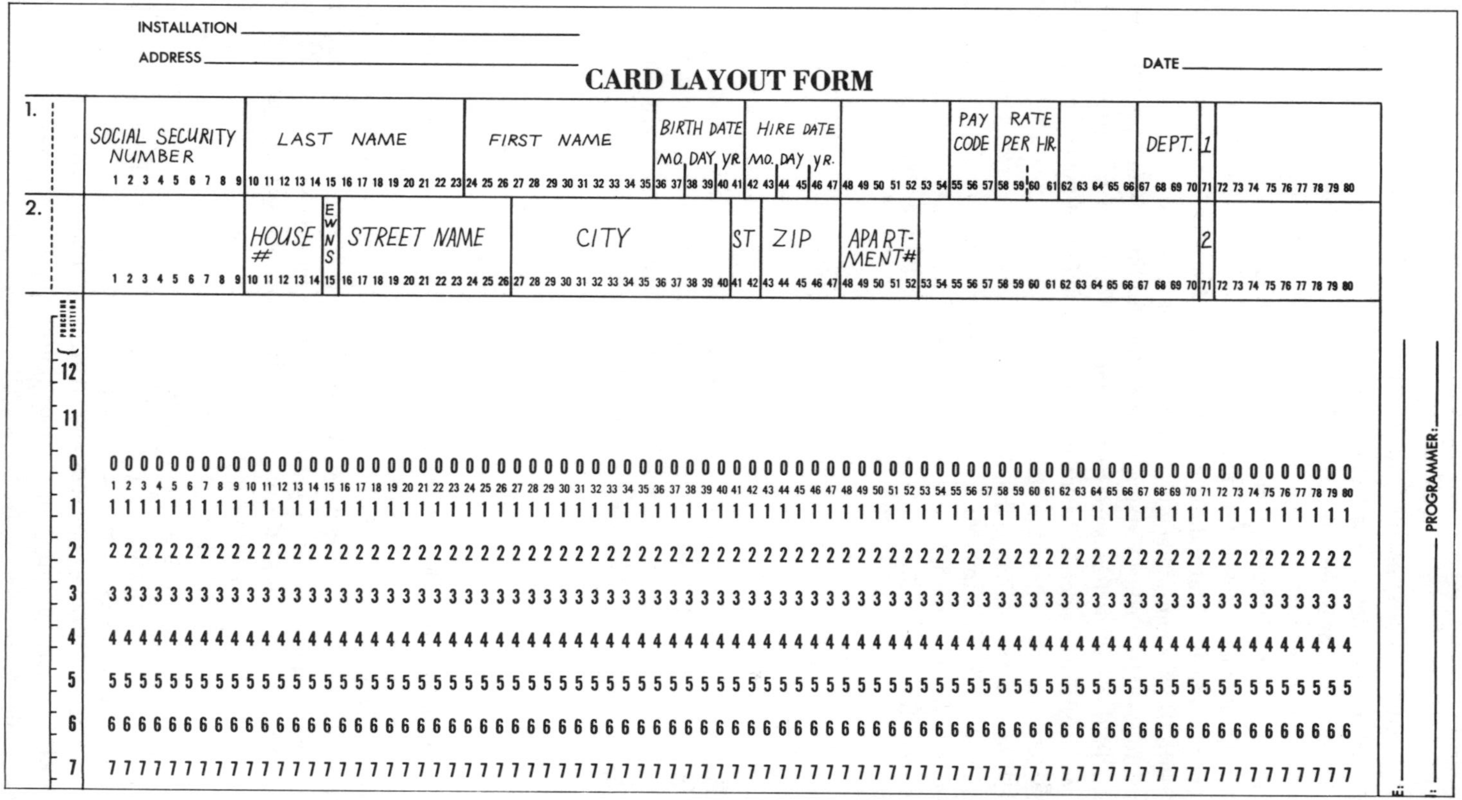

Figure 3-2 Layout for personnel record creation card pairs.

As a result of such analyses, software implementors devised the concept of record blocking, in which (in the case of an output file) multiple data records are collected together until a sufficiently large block is accumulated, at which time the accumulation is transmitted to the file as a single *physical* block of data. In terms of processing, the physical block is said to contain some number of *logical* records; this number is called the blocking factor. On input, the software reads an entire physical block of data at one time, but "doles out" one logical record at a time to the program actually being served by the software.

In addition to saving external space, the blocking technique is more efficient in terms of performance because more information is dealt with each time an external storage device is activated. (It is an axiom of the computer field that the electronic computing speed is significantly greater than the speeds of physical input-output devices). In other words, by blocking a file we manage to get more information into or out of the computer each time we interrupt its computing tasks. It is the interrupting aspect of the input-output process that is so relatively time-consuming because it takes time to set the devices in question into motion.

3.6 Labeled Files

Another software technique applicable only to non-unit-record files is labeling. The file label, a special kind of record that is distinct from any data record, protects a valuable data file from accidental destruction. The file label contains essentially three kinds of information:

1. file-name
2. reel id number
3. expiration date (or creation date plus retention-period).

All output tape handling begins with the reading of the assigned tape to look for a label record. If one is not found, then the tape may be used as an unlabeled output file. If a label record is found, however, the software system compares the current date to the expiration date. Only if the current date is chronologically later than the expiration date may the tape now be used for the output of another file, which will result in the label being rewritten with the same reel id number but a different file-name and expiration date.

Consider a tape file containing all the data for a company's accounts receivable. Obviously this information is very important to the company. If the tape in question were unlabeled, it would be possible for any program to write onto the tape if it were mounted on a tape drive station at the wrong time through human error or carelessness. This act of writing over previous information would destroy the former information—a catastrophe to the company's day-to-day operations.

With labeled tapes, the software system intercedes to protect the integrity of any active labeled file. In our example, we see that any mis-mounting of the labeled accounts receivable tape file could not cause a catastrophe, because the tape label prevents the premature demise of the information contained on the tape.

In general, unlabeled tapes cannot be written onto previously labeled tapes, regardless of whether the expiration date has been reached or not. The reason for this is that an installation goes to considerable trouble to pre-label certain reels of tape and has other unlabeled reels ("scratch tapes") available when needed.

Exercises

1. Arrange the terms *record, field*, and *file* in a diagram to illustrate the proper relationships between them. Choose the punched card as the medium for this depiction.

2. Complete this table in order to see the gain in efficiency of recording on magnetic tape with various block factors. (Assume record size = 120 characters; IRG = inter-record gap length 0.75″; density = 800 bpi.)

Block Factor	Length of Block	Block/IRG Ratio
1	$120/800 = 0.15″$	$0.15/0.75 = 0.20$
2		
5		
10		
15		
20		
30		

3. Can you think of some reasons for using very small block factors?

4

COBOL FILE DESCRIPTIONS

4.1 File Definition Entry

Files are defined in the File Section of the Data Division. Their definition consists of two principal components—an FD entry and its related record description(s). The FD entry (FD stands for File Definition) is defined in general terms in the following way:

FD file-name <u>LABEL RECORDS</u> ARE

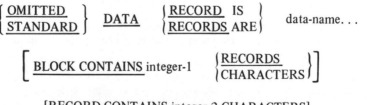

[<u>RECORD</u> CONTAINS integer-2 CHARACTERS]

[<u>RECORDING</u> MODE IS mode] .

As mentioned previously, FD is a reserved word which must appear in Margin A. In practice, FD should appear in card columns 8-9; columns 10-11 must be left blank; the file-name may then appear anywhere beyond column 11, on the same or another card, subject to the constraint of not extending beyond

28

column 72 in any card. The remainder of the entry may be placed in any number of cards within the confines of columns 12-72. The last clause of an FD entry must be followed immediately by a period.

Both the Label Records clause and the Data Records clause are required. In addition, the BLOCK clause is required if the file in question is or will be blocked. In some compilers, there are different implementor-dependent file recording modes. Depending on the computer system and compiler in question, the Recording Mode clause may be required. In the IBM System 360 and RCA Spectra 70, the Recording Mode clause is required to make explicit the user's choice of three different recording modes.

Mode	Description
F	Every record is of constant (fixed) length.
V	Variable-length records; each logical record is preceded by a count control field which is not available for treatment as data (it is used by the data management software).
U	Unblocked records of unspecified length(s).

Though the RECORD CONTAINS clause is never required, it is often used in order to specify a record length that the compiler can use to check against its own calculation of record size. Thus, any later data description error which prevents the attainment of a correct predetermined record size will create a disparity which will be noted in a diagnostic message in the compilation run.

4.1-1 Label Records Clause

The form <u>LABEL</u> <u>RECORDS</u> ARE <u>OMITTED</u> is required for any unlabeled file. The form <u>LABEL</u> <u>RECORDS</u> ARE <u>STANDARD</u> is required for any file which is or will be labeled; in general, mass-storage files must be described by this clause, and unit-record files must not have this form in their FD entry. In the vast world of different computers and COBOL compilers, there are numerous variants and extensions to this clause, none of which is significant enough to cause us to tarry here.

4.1-2 DATA RECORDS Clause

In most compilers, the DATA RECORDS clause is required, because for many years the successive versions of the COBOL standard required it, even though it was little more than a redundant nuisance. Ironically, the latest COBOL standard now makes it optional, but it will be some time before this relaxed standard is implemented and in use. In short, this clause will be treated by us as required (and also as a good object lesson in the futility of some COBOL language standardization efforts). The DATA RECORDS clause consists of an enumeration of each record-name defined as a level-01 data record subsequent to this FD entry and prior to the next file, section, or division definition. We will be discussing levels and record descriptions in section 4.2; examples of complete File Sections may be found in Appendixes C-E. A record-name is simply a data-name at level 01 in the File Section.

4.1-3 BLOCK CONTAINS Clause

Block size may be specified in terms of number of records or number of characters. For unblocked files, this clause is omitted. The form <u>BLOCK</u> CONTAINS integer-1 <u>RECORDS</u> specifies that the physical record size must be adequate to contain integer-1 records.

The form <u>BLOCK</u> CONTAINS integer-1 CHARACTERS is used when the user knows the exact number of characters that make up a physical record. This latter form requires more detailed knowledge of the data-management software in use on a given computer. For example, in using the IBM System 360 recording mode V, the value given as integer-1 must include all characters required as count-control fields.

4.2 Levels of Data

We have seen earlier that data records consist of subdivisions of data called fields. The collection of all related fields is called a record. A collection of all related records is called a file. In COBOL terminology, *item* is used as a synonym for *field*.

Let us discuss in detail the payroll record originally presented in section 3.3. A typical data layout is shown in Figure 4-1.

Name of Employee		Social Security Number	Address			Birth Date		
First	Last		Number	Street	City	Mo	Day	Year

Hire Date			Department	Pay Rate	Year-to-Date-Figures		
						Deductions	
Mo	Day	Year			Gross	FIT	FICA

Figure 4-1 Personnel record layout.

In examining the personnel record layout, we see that several groups exist: Name of Employee consists of First and Last name components; Address consists of 3 parts—Number, Street, and City; both Birth Date and Hire Date have Month, Day, and Year subdivisions; and Deductions includes two detailed fields.

The corresponding COBOL record description, in part, could be written as follows:

```
01   PAYROLL-RECORD.
     02   NAME-OF-EMPLOYEE.
          03   FIRST
          03   LAST
     02   SOCIAL-SECURITY-NUMBER
     02   ADDRESS.
          03   NUMBER
          03   STREET
          03   CITY
     02   BIRTH-DATE.
          03   MO
          03   DA
          03   YR
     02   HIRE-DATE
          03   MM
          03   DD
          03   YY
     02   DEPARTMENT
     02   PAYRATE
     02   YTD-FIGURES.
          03   GROSS
          03   DEDUCTIONS.
               04  FIT
               04  FICA
```

The above COBOL record description is complete except for those fields lacking a period immediately after the data-name; these *fields, which are not subdivided further, are called elementary fields and require a Picture clause to describe the type of data and its size.*

Examination of the progression of level numbers reveals these rules in operation:

1. The most inclusive groupings are indicated by the level number 01. The associated data-name is a record-name.
2. If the level number of the field following a given field is numerically greater than the level of the given field, then the given field is a group item, and the field below it is part of the group.
3. If the level number of the field following a given field is not numerically greater than the level of the given field, then the given field is an elementary item. Consequently, there must be a Picture clause in the description of the given field.

The above rules are valid only for level numbers in the range 01-49. Level number 77 (available only in Working-storage[4]) is essentially a level-01 elementary item. Level number 88 is used only for naming data conditions, a matter deferred to Chapter 8.

4.3 Data Description Entry

The general form of a File Section data description entry is:

level $\begin{cases} \text{data-name-1} \\ \underline{\text{FILLER}} \end{cases}$ [REDEFINES data-name-2] [PICTURE IS depiction]

[OCCURS integer TIMES] [USAGE-clause] [JUSTIFIED-clause] .

We have already seen that each group or elementary item must be defined by an appropriate level number and data-name. Instead of a data-name, the reserved word FILLER may be used, provided there are to be no references to the data area. At level 01 in the File Section, FILLER may not be used as the data-name.

If an item is elementary, there must be a PICTURE clause. If it is not elementary there must not be a PICTURE clause. All the other clauses may be written for any item, as required and subject to their own particular rules, which are specified and elaborated in the remaining sections of this chapter.

Level numbers may be written in Margin A, if desired. The usual practice is to place level 01 in Margin A and all others in Margin B. Every data description begins on a new source card. Data-name-1, FILLER, and any data description clause may not appear in Margin A.

4.4 Types of Data Items

Several types of data items can be described in a COBOL source program. Data types commonly available today in typical computers include binary

---

[4]Or in the Constant Section, if available in the compiler.

numbers, zoned or packed decimal data, edited data, and character strings. Data may also be grouped for consideration on a composite basis.

4.4-1 Group Items

A group item is defined as one having further subdivisions containing one or more elementary items. In addition, a group item may contain other groups. An item is a group item if, and only if, its level number is less than the level number of the immediately succeeding item. If an item is not a group item, then it is an elementary item. A group item is always considered as an unstructured mass of characters without regard to the nature of individual elementary items contained within the group.

4.4-2 Elementary Items

An elementary item is a data item containing no subordinate items; it is always described by means of a PICTURE clause.

Character String Item

A character string item consists of any combination of characters representable in a computer system. Each character is stored in a separate character position. The term *byte* is also used to describe a character position in the form of six or eight binary bits, the number of bits depending on the design of the particular computer system.

Report (Edited) Item

A report item, which represents a number in a special edited form, consists of digits and special editing characters. It must not exceed 30 characters in length. A report item can be used only as a receiving field for numeric data. An example of an edited item is $2,376.82.

Numeric Items

External Decimal Item. Decimal numbers in the System/360 zoned format are called external decimal items. Each digit of a number is represented by a single byte, with the four low-order bits of each eight-bit byte containing the representation of one digit. The four high order bits of each byte are zone bits; the zone bits of the low-order byte represent the sign of the item. The maximum length of an external decimal item is 18 digits. For items whose PICTURE does not contain an S, the sign position is occupied by a bit configuration which is interpreted as positive but does not represent an explicit overpunch. *Overpunch* is a term used to describe a commonly accepted business data-processing practice of combining a 12-row (positive) or 11-row (negative) punch with a digit punch in the rightmost position of a numeric field in punched cards.

Internal Decimal Item. An internal decimal item consisting of numeric characters 0 through 9 plus a sign represents a value not exceeding 18 digits in length. It appears in storage as "packed" decimal. One byte contains two digits with the low-order byte containing the low-order digit followed by the sign of the item. This data format is peculiar to the System 360, RCA Spectra 70, and XDS Sigma series computers.

Binary Item. A binary item may be considered decimally as consisting of numeric characters 0 through 9 plus a sign. The binary data format is extremely compact, inasmuch as the binary number system is employed. Lengths of binary items (in terms of bytes) obey different rules on different computer systems.

4.5 PICTURE Clause

The PICTURE clause specifies a detailed description of an elementary-level data item.

The general format of the PICTURE clause is:

$$\underline{\text{PICTURE}} \ \ \text{IS} \ \ \begin{cases} \text{ch-form} \\ \text{numeric-form} \\ \text{report-form} \end{cases}$$

There are three major types of pictures: the ch-form (sometimes also called alphanumeric-form) describes a character string item; the numeric-form describes a numeric item; and the report-form describes a report (edited) item. For example, X signifies one "character position" in the field, in which any character (value) may be represented. For a larger field, we might write PICTURE XXXXXXX. However, a more convenient form, X(7), is also available. Thus, for repetitions of a given picture character we can write a single Picture character, followed by a number ("replication factor") enclosed in parentheses. The following subsections define the rules for writing the various forms of pictures. Remember, the PICTURE clause states the type and size of data that a field may contain. (For certain numeric data types, the USAGE clause is required also, to determine exactly the type of data).

4.5-1   Ch-form Picture

This Picture option applies to character string items. The PICTURE of a character string item can contain only the character X. An X indicates that the character position may contain any character from the set of allowable characters in the computer.

Examples:

02 NAME-FIELD	PICTURE	X(18).
02 FILLER	PICTURE	X.
02 ADDRESS-FIELD	PICTURE	X(29).

4.5-2   Numeric-form Picture

This option refers to a fixed-point numeric item. The Picture of a numeric item may contain a valid combination of the following characters:

Character Meaning

9   The character 9 indicates that the actual or conceptual digit position contains a numeric character.

V   The character V indicates the position of an assumed decimal point. Since a numeric item cannot contain an actual decimal point, an assumed decimal point is used to provide the compiler with information concerning the scaling alignment of items involved in computations.

S   This character indicates that the item has an operation sign. S must be the first character of any picture in which it appears.

P   This character indicates that there are missing (truncated) digit positions. The P character may only appear exclusively to the right of, or exclusively to the left of, all 9's in the picture.

The tabulation below contains illustrations and explanations of some correct numeric-form pictures.

Picture	Discussion
999	An unsigned 3-digit integral field.
S99999	A signed 4-digit integral field.

Picture	Discussion
S999V99	A signed 5-digit field; the last two digit positions contain the tenths and hundredths digits of the fractional part.
S9(3)V9(2)	Same as above.
999PP	A 3-digit field representing hundreds without retention of the actual tens and units positions.

4.5-3 Report-form Picture

This option refers to a report item. The editing characters that may be combined to describe a report item are as follows:

$$9 \ V \ P \ \cdot \ Z \ * \ CR \ DB \ , \ + \ - \ B \ 0 \ \$$$

The characters 9, V, and P have the same meaning as for a numeric item. The meanings of the other allowable editing characters are presented below.

> The decimal point character (·) specifies that an actual decimal point is to be inserted in the indicated position and the source item is to be aligned accordingly. Numeric character positions to the right of an actual decimal point in a Picture must consist of characters of one type only (i.e., all Z or * or 9 or $ or + or −).

Z The character Z is the zero-suppression character. Each Z in a PICTURE represents a digit position. Leading zeros to be placed in positions defined by Z are suppressed, leaving the position blank. Zero suppression terminates upon encountering the actual decimal point, regardless of the value being edited. A Z cannot appear anywhere to the right of a 9.

* The character * represents a digit position. If the associated digit is a leading zero, an asterisk appears in its place. This practice is called *check protection*, inasmuch as it is often used to prevent tampering with a computer-produced check amount. An asterisk cannot appear anywhere to the right of a 9. Check protection terminates upon encountering the decimal point. After movement of a zero value to the field, it consists of asterisks exclusively, if all digit positions were defined by *.

CR CR and DB are called credit and debit symbols and may appear
DB only at the right end of a picture. These symbols occupy two character positions and indicate that the specified symbol is to

appear in the indicated positions if the value of a source item is negative. If the value is positive or zero, spaces will appear instead. CR and DB and + and − are mutually exclusive.

,   The comma character specfies insertion of a comma between digits; it is counted in the size of the data item but does not represent a digit position. The comma may also appear in conjunction with a floating string, which is described later in this subsection.

+   The characters + or − may appear in a Picture either singly or in a
−   floating string. As a fixed sign control character, the + or − must appear as the last symbol in the Picture. The plus sign indicates that the sign of the item is indicated by either a plus or minus placed in the character position, depending on the algebraic sign of the numeric value placed in the report field. The minus sign indicates that blank or minus is placed in the character position, depending on whether the algebraic sign of the numeric value placed in the report field is positive or negative, respectively.

B   The insertion character B (when not immediately preceded by D) represents a blank position in the edited field. The character B is necessary for this purpose because the entire picture is considered to be one element; blanks are used only as source program element separators except when used in a non-numeric literal.

0   The character zero (0) is also an insertion character, representing a character position in which a zero will appear. In practice, 0's are used in a picture to correspond to P's (omitted zero positions) in the picture of a numeric item when the latter is to be edited into the former. The 0 insertion character does not count in the numeric length of the report item.

A floating string is defined as a leading, continuous series of either $ or + or −, or a string composed of one such character interrupted by one or more insertion characters and/or decimal point. For example:

———B———.99
$$,$$$,$$$
++++
——,———,——
+(8).++
$$,$$$.$$

A floating string containing n + 1 occurrences of $ or + or − defines n digit positions. When a numeric value is moved into a report item, the appropriate character floats from left to right, so that the developed report item has exactly one actual $ or + or − immediately to the left of the most significant nonzero digit, in one of the positions indicated by $ or + or − in the Picture. Blanks are placed in all character positions to the left of the single developed $ or + or −. If the most significant digit appears in a position to the right of positions defined by a floating string, then the developed item contains $ or + or − in the rightmost position of the floating string, and nonsignificant zeros may follow. The presence of a decimal point in a floating string is treated as if all digit positions to the right of the point were indicated by the Picture character 9, with the additional proviso that the field is entirely blank if a zero value is moved to it.

In the following examples, b represents a blank in the developed items.

PICTURE	Numeric Value	Developed Item
+++++·99	14	bb+14·00
$$$999	14	bb$014
−−,−−−,999	−456	bbbbbb−456
$$$$$$	14	bbb$14

When a comma appears to the right of a floating string, the string character floats through the comma in order to be as close to the leading digit as possible.

As shown in the preceding examples, a floating string need not constitute the entire Picture of a report item.

Other rules for a report item Picture are as follows:

1. The appearance of one type of floating string precludes any other floating string.
2. There must be at least one digit-position character.
3. The appearance of a floating sign string or trailing plus or minus insertion characters precludes the appearance of any other of the sign control insertion characters, namely, + − CR DB.
4. The characters to the right of a decimal point up to the end of a Picture, excluding the fixed insertion characters + − CR DB (if present), are subject to the following restrictions:
   a. Only one type of digit position character may appear. That is, Z * 9 and floating-string digit position characters $ + − are mutually exclusive.
   b. If any of the numeric character positions to the right of a decimal point is represented by + or − or $ or Z then all the numeric character positions in the Picture must be represented by the same character.
5. The Picture character 9 can never appear to the left of a floating string. In fact, nothing can precede a floating string.

6. All characters except V and S are counted in the total size of a data item. CR and DB occupy two character positions.

7. A maximum of 30 character positions is allowed in a Picture character string. For example, Picture Z(11) consists of five Picture characters.

8. A Picture must consist of at least one of the characters Z, *, 9 or at least two consecutive appearances of the + or − or $ character.

9. The characters · VS CR and DB can appear only once in a Picture.

The examples in Figure 4-2 illustrate the use of PICTURE to edit data. In each example, a movement of data is implied, as indicated by the column headings.

Source Area		Receiving Area	
PICTURE	Data Value	PICTURE	Edited Data
9(5)	12345	$$$,$$9.99	$12,345.00
9(5)	00123	$$$,$$9.99	$123.00
9(5)	00000	$$$,$$9.99	$0.00
9(4)V9	12345	$$$,$$9.99	$1,234.50
V9(5)	12345	$$$,$$9.99	$0.12
S9(5)	00123	- - - , - - - .99	123.00
S9(5)	-00001	- - - , - - - .99	-1.00
S9(5)	00123	+++++++.99	+123.00
S9(5)	00001	- - - - - - - .99	1.00
9(5)	00123	+++++++.99	+123.00
9(5)	00123	- - - - - - - .99	123.00
S9(5)	12345	$$$$$$$.99CR	$12 345.00
S9(5)	01234	Z(5)+	1234+

Figure 4-2 Editing applications of the PICTURE clause.

4.6 USAGE Clause

The USAGE clause specifies which internal format is used to represent data. It is only relevant to numeric data, and even then may be omitted if desired, in which case the assumed usage format is DISPLAY. All other options of this clause are machine-dependent. In this book, we present the USAGE clause in the form applicable to the IBM System 360, RCA Spectra 70, and XDS Sigma series of computers.

$$\text{USAGE IS} \quad \begin{cases} \text{DISPLAY} \\ \underline{\text{COMPUTATIONAL}} \\ \underline{\text{COMPUTATIONAL-1}} \\ \underline{\text{COMPUTATIONAL-2}} \\ \underline{\text{COMPUTATIONAL-3}} \end{cases}$$

This clause is unusual in that the key word (USAGE) is not required. If the clause is omitted, USAGE DISPLAY is assumed—hence DISPLAY is not underlined in the set of words enclosed above in braces.

In the DISPLAY usage, one numeric digit is contained in one character position (i.e., one byte contains a bit pattern representing a numeric character).

If COMPUTATIONAL usage is specified, data is stored in the form of a binary number of a length dictated by the Picture. (In the Sigma computer series, binary data is required to be integral—therefore V may not appear in the associated Picture.)

If COMPUTATIONAL-3 usage is specified, data is in the packed decimal format. In this format, if there are n 9's in the Picture, then the size of the item is $(n+2)/2$ characters, each of which contains two decimal digits except the last, where only one digit and a representation of the sign are kept.

In the three computer systems previously cited, this packed data format is the most popular type for use in general calculations. In many somewhat earlier style computers (e.g., Univac 1108, IBM 7094, GE 600 series), the computer architecture is essentially exclusively binary, so that the packed decimal data format is not available in those contexts.

In general, the DISPLAY format of numeric data is compatible with all computer lines. Regardless of the formats of numeric data, the same output results will be computed on any machine, given the identical values and formulas. In a way, this is the whole point of COBOL—a machine-independent language common to numerous computers.

The COMPUTATIONAL-1 and COMPUTATIONAL-2 usages declare data in short and long floating-point data formats. No Picture is permitted, as these formats are of a highly specialized and stylized type (fraction and exponent parts). Floating-point numbers, "scientifically-oriented," are in truth approximations carried to about 7 or 16 significant digits, in the short and long formats, respectively; the maximum data value is about 0.72×10^{76}. Short format floating-point data occupies four bytes; long floating-point data occupies eight bytes. These data types are not typically of interest to COBOL users, but their availability can be an enhancement to the utility of COBOL in special circumstances.

A reminder is in order here that the USAGE clause explanations thus far are specifically related to the three EBCDIC computer families cited earlier, namely IBM System 360, RCA Spectra 70, and XDS Sigma. Just to show the caution that must be exercised when dealing with other computer systems, we point out that in the Univac 1108 system, COMPUTATIONAL is taken to be synonymous with DISPLAY; in the 1108, binary data is defined by COMPUTATIONAL-1 and no floating-point COBOL data is available.

In summary, it is reasonable to claim that the USAGE clause is not machine-independent because its various options relate to various hardware-supported data formats. To a much greater extent, all the other data clauses (PICTURE, OCCURS, REDEFINES, and JUSTIFIED) are the same regardless of which computer system is being considered.

4.7 REDEFINES Clause

The REDEFINES clause enables a data area to be given an alternate description. The format of this clause, which must precede any other clauses, if present, is:

REDEFINES data-name-2

When written, the REDEFINES clause must be the first clause in the data description entry.

When an area is redefined, all descriptions of the area remain in effect. Thus, if B and C are two separate items that share the same storage area due to redefinition, the procedure statements MOVE X TO B or MOVE Y TO C could be executed at any point in the program. In the first case, B would assume the value of X and take the form specified by the description of B. In the second case, the same physical area would receive Y according to the description of C.

In the remaining paragraphs, we shall assume for purposes of discussion that data-name-1 is the name of the entry which has the REDEFINES clause. The level number of data-name-2 must be identical to that of data-name-1.

Between data-name-2 and data-name-1 there may be no entries having a lower level number than the level number of data-name-2 and data-name-1. This clause must not be used in level 1 entries in the File Section of the Data Division. Implicit redefinition is provided by the DATA RECORDS clause in the File Description entry. The record description entry for data-name-2 may not contain an OCCURS clause nor may data-name-2 be subordinate to any entry which contains an OCCURS clause. The size of data-name-1 must be equal to that of data-name-2.

We will illustrate the use of this clause in Fig. 4-3 by considering a nine digit input field, SOCIAL-SEC-NUM, which is to be converted to its hyphenated form for output in a report.

```
02      SOCIAL-SEC-NUM      PICTURE        9(9).
02      SS-NO-PARTS         REDEFINES      SOCIAL-SEC-NUM·
        03   SLEFT          PICTURE        999·
        03   SMIDDLE        PICTURE        99·
        03   SRIGHT         PICTURE        9999·
```

Figure 4-3 Illustration of REDEFINES.

We see in Figure 4-3 that the programmer has available the name SOCIAL-SEC-NUM whenever he wants to refer to the entire nine digit field. But, in order to move the three parts separately to output fields which will have hyphens between them, he has devised the alternate names SLEFT, SMIDDLE, and SRIGHT. Note that the size of the group named SS-NO-PARTS is 3 + 2 + 4 = 9, which equals the length of the redefined area.

4.8 OCCURS Clause and Subscripting

The OCCURS clause is used in defining related sets of repeated data, such as tables, lists, and vectors. It specifies the number of times that a data item with the same format is repeated. Data Description clauses associated with an item whose description includes an OCCURS clause apply to each repetition of the item being described. When the OCCURS clause is used, the data-name that is the defining name of the entry must be subscripted whenever it appears in the Procedure Division. If this data-name is the name of a group item, than all data-names belonging to the group must be subscripted whenever they are used. The OCCURS clause must not be used in any Data Description entry having level number 01 or 77. The OCCURS clause has the following format:

OCCURS integer TIMES

Subscripting

Subscripting is the facility for referring to data items in a table or list that have not been assigned individual data-names. Subscripting is determined by the appearance of an OCCURS clause in a data description. If an item has an OCCURS clause or belongs to a group having an OCCURS clause, it must be subscripted whenever it is used in the Procedure Division.

A subscript is a positive nonzero integer whose value determines to which element a reference is being made within a table or list. The subscript may be represented either by an integer literal or a data-name that has an integral value. Whether the subscript is represented by a literal or a data-name, the subscript is enclosed in parentheses and appears after the terminal space of the name of the element. A subscript must be an internal decimal, external decimal, or binary item. (The latter is strongly recommended for the sake of efficiency.)

Example:

```
01   ARRAY.
     03   ELEMENT, OCCURS 3, PICTURE S9 (9) COMPUTATIONAL.
```

The above example would be allocated in storage as shown in Figure 4-4.

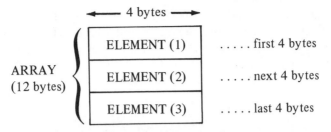

Figure 4-4 Structure of subscripted data.

A data-name may not be subscripted if it is being used for any of the following functions:

1. When it is being used as a subscript.
2. When it appears as the defining name of a Data Description entry.
3. When it appears as data-name-2 in a REDEFINES clause.

Within the three rectangles of Figure 4-4, which represent the three occurrences of ELEMENT, we see the form that subscripted references must take to refer to each of the data fields. These references may only appear in the Procedure Division, when data is manipulated by the various statements available in COBOL. For example, we might do the following at some point in the logic of the program:

MOVE 1 TO ELEMENT (3).

We will have more illustrations of subscripting in our later discussion of the Procedure Division. There is a more complex form of the OCCURS clause, which permits the number of occurrences to be variable, with the exact number of occurrences at any instant taken to be the current value of a designated data item. This form is:

OCCURS [integer-1 TO] integer-2 TIMES

DEPENDING ON data-name

Multiple subscripts are required when multiple OCCURS clauses govern a data field. For example:

```
01  COLLECTION.
    02  SUBSET OCCURS 5.
        03  ROW OCCURS 4.
            04  BUNCH OCCURS 7.
```

In the group item called COLLECTION, there are 5 x 4 x 7 different fields called BUNCH, and it takes three subscripts to locate any specific one, because there are OCCURS clauses in effect at two group levels containing BUNCH, plus one OCCURS clause describing BUNCH at level 04. Three OCCURS clauses is the maximum applicable to any field.

Examples:

BUNCH (1, 1, 1)
BUNCH (I, J, K)
BUNCH (2, TALLY, X-ROW).

Returning to our illustration, we observe that ROW references must include two subscripts, while SUBSET references require exactly one subscript whenever referenced.

4.9 JUSTIFIED Clause

Non-numeric elementary items (ch-form Pictures) may include the following clause in their descriptions:

<u>JUSTIFIED RIGHT</u>

Inclusion of this clause reverses the normal method of moving data to the field. Instead of moving data character by character, starting at the left of the sending field, movement starts at the right end of the sending field and goes into the rightmost character position of the receiving field. The process continues, proceeding in the leftward direction to obtain additional sending characters. For a more detailed discussion, refer to the MOVE statement explanation.

Exercises

1. Write the FD entry for
   a. a file that is assigned to a card-reader device
   b. a file on unlabeled magnetic tape, logical record size 100 characters, physical record size 600 characters.
2. Write pictures for the following types of data fields.
   a. numeric data, capable of containing a maximum value of 999.9 and also capable of being signed algebraically.
   b. an unsigned numeric field having ten digits, of which two are reserved to represent a fractional component.

    c. a report field suitable for presenting the data in (b), with commas separating each group of 3 digits left of the decimal point.

    d. a 5-character non-numeric field.

3. Review the data descriptions of the sample programs in Appendixes C, D, and E to get a good grasp on the techniques in defining data for use by procedural statements. (If you have any questions on this subject, *now* is the time to ask your instructor.)

4. Of the several FD-entry clauses, which ones are actually required by the COBOL compiler to which you have access? Does this vary by type of device? Prepare your answer in the form of a table listing device (assignment) types in different columns, with different rows for each clause (RECORDING, LABEL, etc.).

5. Explain:

    a. The relationship between level numbers in the range 01–49.

    b. The relationship between level 77 and 01.

    c. The relationship between level numbers and the PICTURE clause.

6. If the level of a group item is k, what is the level of the next data item?

7. On the IBM 360, what type of data is defined by COMPUTATIONAL-3?

8. On the IBM 360 and RCA Spectra 70, binary data is defined by USAGE _____.

9. Specify the length (in bytes) of IBM 360 "packed decimal" data having the following Pictures:

    a. S9

    b. S9(7)

    c. S9(3)V9

    d. S9(3)V9(3)

    e. S9(4)V99

5

THE WORKING-STORAGE SECTION

5.1 Purpose of Working-storage

Descriptions of files and records are stated in the File Section. For any active file, exactly one record is available in the computer at any given time.

When processing data, it is usually necessary to maintain additional data in memory on a long-term basis. For example, as file records are processed (read) one at a time, values found therein may be added to a data item in order to form a total. The Working-storage section includes data which is unrelated to files. It is used to include tables of values, report-heading text information and other data fields that are needed in the processing steps.

Working-storage data descriptions are similar to data descriptions in the File Section, except that there are no FD entries. In addition to levels 01-49, level 77 may be used to define data that is not part of a group structure. Therefore, level 77 always describes an elementary item. All level 77 items must appear before any other levels in Working-storage.

In Working-storage, the VALUE clause may be used in order to establish initial (or constant) values in elementary items. The VALUE clause may not be used in the File Section, because values are found in input records (or created for output records) during the course of reading from (or writing to) a file.

5.2 VALUE Clause

The format of the VALUE clause is:

$$\underline{\text{VALUE}} \text{ IS } \begin{Bmatrix} \text{literal} \\ \text{figurative-constant} \end{Bmatrix}$$

This clause may only appear in Working-storage in the description of an elementary item. The choice of the operand (i.e., literal or figurative constant) must conform to the type of the data field. For a numeric field, the literal must be numeric, or the figurative constant ZERO may be used. For a non-numeric item (ch-form Picture), the literal must be non-numeric (i.e., enclosed in quotation marks), or figurative-constants other than ZERO may be employed.

The VALUE clause is prohibited in several cases:

1. In the description of an item governed by an OCCURS clause.

2. In the description of a report (edited) item.

3. In the description of an item having a REDEFINES clause or subordinate to an item having a REDEFINES clause.

5.3 An Example of Working-storage

Figure 5-1 shows coding for Working-storage requirements of a small program. The program of which this is a part is designed to produce a form letter addressed to the persons whose two-letter standard Post Office state designations are included in a file of pertinent address data. The problem is, in part, to do a table look-up so that the full state spelling will appear in the printed address. Consequently, a set of tables is required. In Figure 5-1, we see how OCCURS, REDEFINES, and VALUE clauses can be used to establish the necessary tables in storage, even though at first thought those three clauses seem to be mutually prohibited by rules of COBOL language.

In Figure 5-1, group item STATES contains six fifteen-character items, each consisting of the thirteen-character state name and the two letter code (in the rightmost two character positions).

Superimposed over this same area, by means of redefinition are six group items (LONG-AND-SHORT) 15 characters long. In this case, the leftmost 13 characters are available through use of the name LONG and an appropriate subscript; the two-letter state codes are likewise available through use of the name SHORT (also subscripted).

Exercises

1. Why is the VALUE clause meaningless (prohibited) in the File Section for any elementary item?

2. Point out the offense, if any, in each of the following program excerpts.

   a. 07 SAM PICTURE X (17) VALUE 3500.

   b. 03 B VALUE 17 PICTURE 99.

COBOL PROGRAM SHEET

Form No. X28-1464-1 U/M 050
Printed in U.S.A.

System								
Program				Graphic	Ø	O	Card Form #	Sheet of
Programmer		Date		Punch	LETTER	DIGIT		* Identification 73 [ ] 80

| SEQUENCE | | | | | |
(PAGE) 3 4	(SERIAL) 6 7	A 8	B 12		
0030	10	WORKING-STORAGE SECTION.
	020	77 I PICTURE S99 COMPUTATIONAL VALUE ZERO.
	030	01 STATES.
	040	02 FILLER PICTURE X(15) VALUE 'CALIFORNIA CA'.
	050	02 FILLER PICTURE X(15) VALUE 'NEVADA NV'.
	060	02 FILLER PICTURE X(15) VALUE 'NEW MEXICO NM'.
	070	02 FILLER PICTURE X(15) VALUE 'OREGON OR'.
	080	02 FILLER PICTURE X(15) VALUE 'WASHINGTON WA'.
	990	02 FILLER PICTURE X(15) VALUE 'ARIZONA AZ'.
	100	TABLE REDEFINES STATES.
	110	02 LONG-AND-SHORT OCCURS 6.
	120	03 LONG PICTURE X(13).
	130	03 SHORT PICTURE XX.

* A standard card form, IBM electro C61897, is available for punching source statements from this form.

Figure 5-1 Example of data table.

c. 04 C VALUE 17 PICTURE S9.

d. 03 D VALUE ZERO PICTURE ZZZ.

e. 05 NAME REDEFINES NAME PICTURE X VALUE 'P'.

3. Define a typical tax-rate table in COBOL so that the appropriate rate may be accessed using a subscript based on the net income range.

6

THE PROCEDURE DIVISION

6.1. Overview

The Procedure Division contains statements which embody the logic and processing steps desired by the programmer. When compiled successfully, user-written statements control the execution of the computer.

The three major classifications in which Procedural statements may be classified are:

1. Imperative statements
2. Conditional statements
3. Compiler-directing statements

Each statement consists of a reserved word (verb) and its proper operands.

The Procedure Division is organized into sections and paragraphs; paragraphs consist of one or more sentences; a sentence consists of one or more statements terminated by a period.

Paragraphs or sections have names; collectively, these are referred to as procedure-names which are used as operands of certain procedural statements, such as the PERFORM or GO TO statements.

6.2 Section-names

A section-name consists of an element not exceeding 30 characters in length. The name may consist of any combination of letters, digits, and embedded hyphens but may not be a reserved word. A procedure-name may consist exclusively of digits. However, the author recommends that the best policy is to eschew purely digital names, since an alphanumeric section-name can better convey a symbolic idea of the purpose of the section. When a section is defined, the name is written in Margin A, followed by one or more spaces, followed by the reserved word SECTION. The word SECTION is immediately followed by a period. In referring to a section (in a GO TO statement, for example), the word SECTION is *not* included, and the reference to the name appears in Margin B. A section includes all subsequent paragraphs, up to the next section definition or the end of the program.

6.3 Paragraph-names

The rule for naming a paragraph is like that for sections, except that the name is immediately followed by a period (rather than the reserved word SECTION). When a procedure-name is defined, the name is written in Margin A. At all other times (references to the name), the procedure-name must not appear in Margin A.

6.4 Imperative Statements

A statement is imperative if it can be executed and has only one possible outcome. This distinction becomes clear in contrast to a conditional statement, whose outcome is uncertain. For example, an IF statement causes a data-to-data comparison to be made; the outcome may be either a true condition or a false condition—and the resultant program path is dependent on which state results from the comparison.

The following is a list of imperative statement types.

OPEN
WRITE   (without the INVALID KEY option)
CLOSE
ACCEPT
DISPLAY
Arithmetic Statements   (without the SIZE ERROR option)
MOVE
EXAMINE
GO TO
ALTER
PERFORM
STOP

EXIT
SORT
RELEASE

6.5 Conditional Statements

Conditional statements are the following:

IF
READ
Arithmetic Statements   (with the SIZE ERROR option)
RETURN

6.6 Functional Classification of Statements

COBOL statements may also be classified by related functions. We can tabulate statements in the following categories:

Comparison Statement
  IF
Arithmetic Statements
  ADD   MULTIPLY
  SUBTRACT   DIVIDE
  COMPUTE
Input-Output Statements
  OPEN   READ
  CLOSE   WRITE
  ACCEPT   DISPLAY
Data Manipulation Statements
  MOVE   EXAMINE
Program Path Control Statements
  GO TO   STOP
  ALTER   EXIT
  PERFORM
Compiler-Directing Statements
  USE   ENTER
  NOTE   INCLUDE
Sort Statements
  RELEASE   RETURN   SORT

We are now ready to begin learning the details of the syntax and meanings of statements.

6.7 OPEN Statement

The OPEN statement must be executed in order to commence file processing. The general format of an OPEN statement is:

$$\text{OPEN} \quad \left\{ \text{mode} \quad \left\{ \text{file-name} \quad [\text{option}] \right\} \quad \ldots \right\} \ldots$$

where: mode may be any of the reserved words INPUT, OUTPUT, INPUT-OUTPUT (or I-O); option is defined by

$$\left\{ \begin{array}{l} \underline{\text{REVERSED}} \\ \text{WITH } \underline{\text{NO}} \ \underline{\text{REWIND}} \end{array} \right\}$$

To interpret this fairly complicated syntax, we can state that an OPEN statement lists any number of file-names, preceded collectively or individually by a reserved word required to state the type of processing (input, output, or combined input-output). Any file-name may be followed by an option, if the file is assigned to a tape device. Such options include the NO REWIND option or the REVERSED option.

The NO REWIND option permits a file to be processed beginning at a point other than the beginning of the physical tape. On computers which have the read-in-reverse capability for tape files, the REVERSED option can be used. The REVERSED option implies the NO REWIND option automatically. For an input file, opening initiates reading the file's first records into memory, so that subsequent READ statements may be executed without waiting. For an output file, opening makes available a record area for development of one record, which will be transmitted to the assigned output device upon the execution of a WRITE statement. Failure to precede (in terms of time sequence) file reading or writing by the execution of an OPEN statement is a serious execution-time error which will cause abnormal termination of a program run.

6.8 READ Statement

The format of a READ statement is:

<u>READ</u> file-name   [<u>INTO</u> data-name]   AT <u>END</u> imperative statement...

The READ statement makes available the next logical data record of the designated file from the assigned device. Since at some time the end-of-file will be encountered, the user must include the AT END clause. The reserved word END is followed by any number of imperative statements, all of which are executed only if the end-of-file situation arises. The last statement in the AT END series must be followed by a period to indicate the end of the series. Normally, when a data record to be read exists, execution of the READ statement is immediately followed by execution of the statement after the period which terminates the series of imperative statements.

Recalling that in some cases there may be several different types of records in one file (see section 3.4), we understand that there could be two or more different record descriptions (level 01) in the associated File Definition. (Recall from section 4.7 that the DATA RECORDS clause implies redefinition of all a file's records into a single data area.) The user must be able to distinguish between the types of records that are possible, in order to determine exactly which type is currently available. This requirement can be achieved by a data comparison, using the IF statement to test a field which has a unique value for each type of record. The INTO option permits the user to specify that a copy of the data record is to be placed into a designated data field immediately after the READ statement. The data-name must not be defined in the file itself.

6.9 WRITE Statement

The format of a WRITE statement is:

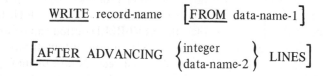

Ignoring the AFTER ADVANCING option for the moment, we proceed to explain the main functions of the WRITE statement. We would do well to begin with a pair of warnings. In COBOL, all file output is achieved by execution of the WRITE statement. Depending on the device assigned, "written" output may take the form of printed matter, magnetic recording on tape or disk, or punched cards. The second warning, when heeded, avoids a frequent error committed by neophytes. The user should observe that you READ file-name, but you WRITE record-name. Record-name must be one of the level 01 records defined for an output file.

If the data to be output has been developed in Working-storage or in another area (for example, in an input file's record area), the FROM option permits the user to stipulate that the designated data (data-name-1) is to be copied into the record-name area, and output from there. The AFTER ADVANCING option, which is restricted to line printer output files, permits the programmer to control the line spacing on the paper in the printer. In this case, it is assumed (on XDS Sigma, RCA Spectra 70, and IBM System 360) that the first character position of the output record is available for storing a line-control character devised from the specified integer or the value of the one-byte field designated by data-name-2. Line printer spacing-control characters should be taken from the following list, if data-name-2 is the form used:

blank	single spacing
0	double spacing (one blank line after last line)
—	triple spacing (two blank lines after last line)
1	start at top of next page

In this case, the programmer has the responsibility of controlling the content of data-name-2.

If the integer number-of-lines form is used in an AFTER ADVANCING clause, values of 1, 2, and 3 call for single, double, or triple spacing. The value 0 is used to start at the top of the next page. Details of the AFTER ADVANCING clause vary in the compilers provided by various other manufacturers on other computer systems. Most of these other systems do not use the first character of the record area to control line spacing, nor do they accept the form AFTER ADVANCING 0 LINES. Instead, we find conventions such as:

- AFTER ADVANCING TO TOP OF PAGE (GE-400)
- AFTER ADVANCING 100 LINES (Univac 1108)—because the value 100 is more than the page line capacity, it forces the start of a new page.

In the three systems toward which this book is primarily oriented, it is necessary to take care that, if a print file is constructed by means of WRITE statements employing the AFTER ADVANCING option, *all* WRITE statements for the file use the option. Violation of this warning is not detected by the compiler and results in a serious execution-time error. This error causes abnormal termination of a program run in such an obscure way that ready diagnosis will usually prove impractical.

Further cautionary notes follow:

1. There is no *separate* AFTER ADVANCING statement; it is permitted only as a clause which forms part of a printer WRITE statement.
2. There is no provision for the singular spelling of the word LINES in the After Advancing clause. WRITE record-name AFTER ADVANCING 1 LINES is acceptable COBOL, if poor English.

6.10 CLOSE Statement

The format of the CLOSE Statement is:

Upon completion of the processing of a file, a CLOSE statement must be executed to cause the software system to make the proper disposition of the device. Whenever a file is closed or has never been opened, READ or WRITE statements cannot be executed properly.

In the CLOSE statement, any number of file-names may appear. For tape files, either the NO REWIND or LOCK option may immediately follow the file name. These options have the following implications:

1. NO REWIND—the normal tape rewinding action is suppressed.
2. LOCK—the tape is rewound and then automatically unloaded for removal from the tape drive. (This action is performed by the computer operator.)

For convenience in processing parts of multi-reel tape files, the file-name in a CLOSE statement may be followed by the reserved word REEL or UNIT, in order to advance to the next reel immediately. In this case, neither the No Rewind nor Lock options is necessary.

6.11 DISPLAY Statement

The DISPLAY statement provides a simple means of outputting low-volume data without the complexities of File Definition. The format of the DISPLAY statement is:

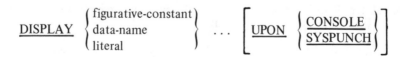

When the UPON suffix is omitted, it is understood that output is to be printed on the Standard Display device for the particular compiler in question. In the System 360 and Spectra 70 COBOL compilers, the standard display device is the on-line high-speed line printer.[5] In nearly all other systems, the standard Display

---

[5]In some very sophisticated operating environments, printing may be deferred and the information temporarily recorded on disk or tape. Ultimately, however, the system will discharge the data on a high-speed line printer.

device is the low-speed console typewriter. The UPON option is not implemented in some systems, such as the XDS Sigma and Univac 1108 COBOL compilers. (If it is implemented, it merely permits the user to employ an alternate symbolic name for the console typewriter.)

In the 360 and Spectra 70 systems, UPON CONSOLE directs that output is to be typed, usually so that the computer operator may read it. UPON SYSPUNCH directs the output to the system's card punch device. In each of these cases, the maximum total number of characters to be output is 72. In the case of card punching, the compiler will cause the last eight card positions (columns 73-80) to contain the program-identification as specified in the PROGRAM-ID paragraph. Values output are literals, figurative-constants (punched as one character), or data fields, converted from binary or packed formats to zoned format, if applicable. Negative data is output in conformance to the overpunched sign convention—for example, the output from the statement

$$\text{DISPLAY} \quad \text{SPACE} \quad -24.$$

would be three characters:

1. a blank or space character
2. the character 2
3. the character M, equivalent to $\overline{4}$, i.e., an 11 zone and a 4 digit punch combined

6.12 ACCEPT Statement

The ACCEPT statement is used to enter data in the computer on a low-volume basis, from either punched cards or operator key-in at the typewriter console. The format of the ACCEPT statement is:

$$\underline{\text{ACCEPT}} \quad \text{data-name} \quad \left[\underline{\text{FROM}} \quad \underline{\text{CONSOLE}}\right]$$

In the System 360 and Spectra 70 systems, omission of FROM CONSOLE implies that input is from SYSIN, which is normally the card reader.[6] One card (or equivalent data) is read, and as many characters as necessary (depending on the size of the named data field) are moved, without change, to the indicated field. When FROM CONSOLE is stated, input is keyed-in at the console typewriter by the operator. In most other systems, only the form ACCEPT data-name is available for operator-keyed input. When input is to be accepted from the console, execution consists of the following steps:

[6] It is possible that SYSIN (or SYSIP T) be assigned to tape or disk, in which case the data is in the form of "copies" or images of cards 80 characters in length.

1. A system-generated message code is typed automatically.
2. Execution is suspended.
3. When a proper operator response is received, the program stores the acquired data in the field designated by data-name, and normal execution proceeds.

When an ACCEPT statement is executed for input from the SYSIN device, and there is an active (presently open) file assigned to the same device, the results are generally unpredictable, because the input-output software generally will have read ahead into the SYSIN data stream (recall our discussion of buffering in section 2.4-2).

6.13 MOVE Statement

The MOVE statement causes data to be moved from one field to another. In a numeric-to-numeric move, when the descriptions of the sending field and receiving field differ, conversion (and digit alignment) take place. When non-numeric data (group or character string items) are moved to another non-numeric data field, another set of rules governs the movement on a character-by-character basis. When numeric data is moved to a group or character string item, the move is treated as strictly non-numeric in all respects. Finally, an important class of moves involves sending numeric fields to report (edited) fields, in which case the editing defined in the receiving field's Picture controls the development of the receiving field. (Refer to section 4.5-3; review Figure 4-2.)

The format of the MOVE statement is:

$$\underline{\text{MOVE}} \quad \left\{ \begin{array}{l} \text{figurative-constant} \\ \text{literal} \\ \text{data-name-1} \end{array} \right\} \quad \underline{\text{TO}} \quad \text{data-name-2} \ldots$$

Note that multiple receiving fields are permitted, so that movement of the same field or value to more than one place can be expressed in one long statement. Figure 6-1 summarizes the legality of combinations of source data and receiving fields. Where a blank is shown, the move is illegal (prohibited by the compiler); letters C, E, or N indicate that the move is done in a character, edited, or numeric fashion, respectively.

Move methods C and N are explained in Sections 6.13-1 and 6.13-2.

6.13-1 Character-to-character Moves

Source data (e.g. data-name-1) is stored in the receiving area, and left justified unless the receiving item is an elementary character-string item having a

Source Data	Receiving Field					
	BI	ID	ED	RE	CH	GR
ZERO or numeric literal	N	N	N	E	C	C
BI (binary field)	N	N	N	E	C	C
ID (internal decimal)	N	N	N	E	C	C
ED (external decimal)	N	N	N	E	C	C
RE (report edited)					C	C
Non-numeric literal[7]					C	C
CH (character string)					C	C
GR (group item)					C	C

Figure 6-1 Permissible MOVE statements.

JUSTIFIED RIGHT clause. If the receiving field is shorter in length than the source field, the number of characters moved is equal to the length of the receiving field. If the source field is shorter, the characters are moved from the source field, and the remainder of the receiving field is filled with spaces. Figure 6-2 illustrates several MOVE results.

Figure 6-2 Character-to-character moves.

6.13-2 Numeric-to-numeric Moves

If the receiving field has a larger scale factor (more 9's to right of V in the Picture) than the sending field, enough zero digits are created at the end of the sending field in order to align the data properly with respect to the assumed decimal point of the receiving field. Similarly, leading zeros are generated when the receiving field has more digit positions to the left of the assumed decimal point than does the receiving field. On the other hand, when the receiving field is shorter at either the left or right side of the assumed decimal point position, truncation (loss of excess digits) occurs. On the left, truncation of non-zero digits is called *loss of significance.*

[7]Includes figurative constants other than ZERO.

Figure 6-3 illustrates typical numeric-to-numeric moves.

Source field		Received field	
Picture	Value	Picture	Value
S9(5)	12345	S9(6)	012345
S9(5)V9	01015¦6	S9(5)	01015
SV999	¦375	S9V99	0¦37
S9(5)	86092	S9(4)V99	6092¦00
S9	4	SV9	¦0

Figure 6-3   Numeric moves.

6.14   EXAMINE Statement

The EXAMINE statement has the following two formats:

Option 1

EXAMINE data-name TALLYING
$\left\{ \begin{array}{l} \underline{ALL} \\ \underline{LEADING} \\ \underline{UNTIL} \ \underline{FIRST} \end{array} \right\}$
'character-1'

[REPLACING BY 'character-2']

Option 2

EXAMINE data-name REPLACING
$\left\{ \begin{array}{l} \underline{ALL} \\ \underline{LEADING} \\ \underline{UNTIL} \ \underline{FIRST} \\ \underline{FIRST} \end{array} \right\}$
'character-1'

BY 'character-2'

The data-name in each option must refer to a data item whose USAGE is DISPLAY. Character-1 and character-2 must be enclosed in quotation marks to indicate that they are single-character non-numeric literals and they must be members of the set of allowable characters for the data item. When the Option 1 EXAMINE statement is used, a count made of the number of occurrences of the specified character-1 in data-name replaces the value of the special binary data item TALLY. TALLY may also be used as a data-name in other procedural statements.

The TALLY count depends on which of the following three TALLYING options is employed:

1. If ALL is specified, all occurrences of character-1 in the data item are counted.
2. If LEADING is specified, the count represents the number of occurrences of character-1 prior to encountering a character other than character-1. Examination proceeds from left to right.
3. If UNTIL FIRST is specified, the count represents the number of characters other than character-1 encountered prior to the first occurrence of character-1. Examination proceeds from left to right.

When the REPLACING option is used (either in Option 1 or Option 2), the replacement of characters depends on which of the following four REPLACING options is employed:

1. If ALL is specified, character-2 is substituted for each occurrence of character-1.
2. If LEADING is specified, the substitution of character-2 for character-1 terminates when a character other than character-1 is encountered, or when the right-hand boundary of the data item is reached. Examination proceeds from left to right.
3. If UNTIL FIRST is specified, the substitution of character-2 terminates as soon as the first character-1 is encountered or when the right-hand boundary is reached. Examination proceeds from left to right.
4. If FIRST is specified, only the first occurrence of character-1 is replaced by character-2. Examination proceeds from left to right.

Sample EXAMINE statements showing the effect of each statement on the associated data item and the TALLY are shown in Fig. 6-4.

Statement	Item X Before	Item X After	TALLY Result
EXAMINE X TALLYING ALL '*'	****3.67	unchanged	4
EXAMINE X TALLYING ALL '*' REPLACING BY 'b'	****3.67	bbbb3.67	4
EXAMINE X REPLACING LEADING '0' BY '*'	00061.00	***61.00	unchanged

Figure 6-4 EXAMINE statement results.

6.15   Arithmetic Statements

There are five arithmetic verbs: ADD, SUBTRACT, MULTIPLY, DIVIDE, and COMPUTE. Any arithmetic statement may be either imperative or conditional. When an arithmetic statement includes an ON SIZE ERROR specification, the entire statement is termed conditional, because the occurrence of the size error condition is data-dependent. A conditional statement must always be the last statement in a sentence. An example of a conditional arithmetic statement is:

ADD 1 TO RECORD-COUNT, ON SIZE ERROR MOVE ZERO TO
RECORD-COUNT, DISPLAY 'ANOTHER HUNDRED TRANSACTIONS'
UPON CONSOLE.

Note that, if a size error occurs (in this case, it is apparent that RECORD-COUNT has Picture 99, and cannot hold a value of 100), both the MOVE and DISPLAY statements are executed. Otherwise, the MOVE and DISPLAY statements are not executed. The three statement components that may appear in arithmetic statements (GIVING option, ROUNDED option, and SIZE ERROR option) are discussed in detail in 6.15-1 through 6.15-3.

Rules for Arithmetic Statements

1. All data-names used in arithmetic statements must be elementary numeric data items that are defined in the Data Division of the program except when they are the operands of the GIVING or CORRESPONDING options. The automatically defined binary item TALLY may also be used.
2. Decimal point alignment is supplied automatically throughout the computations.
3. Intermediate-result fields generated for the evaluation of arithmetic expressions assure the accuracy of the result field except where high-order truncation is necessary.

The ROUNDED and SIZE ERROR options apply to all five arithmetic statements. The GIVING option applies to all arithmetic statements except COMPUTE.

6.15-1   SIZE ERROR Option

If, after decimal-point alignment and any low-order truncation, the value of a calculated result exceeds the largest value which the receiving field is capable of holding, a size error condition exists.

The format of the SIZE ERROR option is:

ON SIZE ERROR imperative statement . . .

If the SIZE ERROR option is present, and a size error condition arises, the value of the resultant data-name is not predictable, and the series of imperative statements specified for the condition is executed. If the SIZE ERROR option has not been specified and a size error condition arises, no assumption should be made about the final result; but the program flow is not interrupted.

An arithmetic statement, if written with a SIZE ERROR option, is not an imperative statement. Rather, it is a conditional statement and is prohibited in contexts where only imperative statements are allowed.

6.15-2   ROUNDED Option

If, after decimal-point alignment, the number of places calculated for the result is greater than the number of places in the data item that is to be set equal to the calculated result, truncation occurs unless the ROUNDED option has been specified.

When the ROUNDED option is specified, the least significant digit of the resultant data-name has its value increased by 1 whenever the most significant digit of the excess is greater than or equal to 5.

Rounding of a computed negative result is performed by rounding the absolute value of the computed result and then making the final result negative.

Figure 6-5 illustrates the relationship between a calculated result and the value stored in an item that is to receive the calculated result, with and without rounding.

Calculated Result		Item to Receive Calculated Result	
	PICTURE	Value After Rounding	Value After Truncating
−12.36	S99V9	−12.4	−12.3
8.432	9V9	8.4	8.4
35.6	99V9	35.6	35.6
65.6	S99V	66	65
.0055	SV999	.006	.005

Figure 6-5   Illustration of rounding.

6.15-3   GIVING Option

If the GIVING option is written, the value of the data-name that follows the word GIVING is made equal to the calculated result of the arithmetic operation.

The data-name that follows GIVING is not used in the computation and may be a report item. If the GIVING option is not written, the operand following the words ADD TO, SUBTRACT FROM, MULTIPLY BY, or DIVIDE INTO statement is also used in the computation and is then made equal to the result.

6.15-4   ADD Statement

The ADD statement adds together two or more numeric values and stores the resulting sum. The ADD statement format is:

$$\underline{\text{ADD}} \quad \begin{Bmatrix} \text{numeric-literal} \\ \text{data-name-1} \end{Bmatrix} \quad \cdots$$

$$\begin{Bmatrix} \underline{\text{TO}} \\ \underline{\text{GIVING}} \end{Bmatrix} \quad \text{data-name-n} \quad [\underline{\text{ROUNDED}}] \quad [\text{SIZE-ERROR-clause}]$$

When the TO option is used, the values of all the data-names (including *data-name-n*) and literals in the statement are added, and the resulting sum replaces the value of *data-name-n*. At least two data-names and/or numeric literals must follow the word ADD when the GIVING option is written.

The following are examples of Option 1 ADD statements:

ADD INTEREST, DEPOSIT TO BALANCE

ADD REGULAR-TIME OVERTIME GIVING NEW-WEEKLY

The first statement would result in the total sum of INTEREST, DEPOSIT, and BALANCE being placed at BALANCE, while the second would result in the sum of REGULAR-TIME and OVERTIME being placed at the location NEW-WEEKLY.

6.15-5   SUBTRACT Statement

The SUBTRACT statement subtracts one or more numeric data items from a specified item and stores the difference.

The SUBTRACT statement format is:

$$\underline{\text{SUBTRACT}} \quad \begin{Bmatrix} \text{data-name-1} \\ \text{numeric-literal-1} \end{Bmatrix} \quad \cdots \quad \underline{\text{FROM}}$$

$$\left\{ \begin{array}{l} \text{data-name-m} \quad [\underline{\text{GIVING}} \quad \text{data-name-n}] \\ \text{numeric literal-m} \quad \underline{\text{GIVING}} \quad \text{data-name-n} \end{array} \right\}$$

$$[\underline{\text{ROUNDED}}] \quad [\text{SIZE-ERROR-clause}]$$

The effect of the SUBTRACT statement is to sum the values of all the operands that precede FROM and then to subtract that sum from the value of the item following FROM.

The result (difference) is stored in data-name-n, if there is a GIVING option. Otherwise, the result is stored in data-name-m. All data-name operands must be numeric fields except that the name in the GIVING option may be a report item.

6.15-6 MULTIPLY Statement

The MULTIPLY statement computes the product of two numeric data items and stores the product.

The format of the MULTIPLY statement is:

$$\underline{\text{MULTIPLY}} \quad \left\{ \begin{array}{l} \text{data-name-1} \\ \text{numeric-literal-1} \end{array} \right\}$$

$$\underline{\text{BY}} \quad \left\{ \begin{array}{l} \text{data-name-2} \quad [\underline{\text{GIVING}} \quad \text{data-name-3}] \\ \text{numeric-literal-2} \quad \underline{\text{GIVING}} \quad \text{data-name-3} \end{array} \right\}$$

$$[\underline{\text{ROUNDED}}] \quad [\underline{\text{SIZE-ERROR}}\text{-clause}]$$

When the GIVING option is omitted, the second operand must be a data-name; the product replaces the value of data-name-2. For example, a new BALANCE value is computed by the statement MULTIPLY 1.03 BY BALANCE. (Since this order might seem somewhat unnatural, it is recommended that GIVING always be written.)

6.15-7 DIVIDE Statement

The DIVIDE statement computes a quotient of two numeric values and stores it. The format of the DIVIDE statement is:

$$\underline{\text{DIVIDE}} \quad \left\{ \begin{array}{l} \text{data-name-1} \\ \text{numeric-literal-1} \end{array} \right\} \quad \left\{ \begin{array}{l} \underline{\text{BY}} \\ \underline{\text{INTO}} \end{array} \right\} \quad \left\{ \begin{array}{l} \text{data-name-2} \\ \text{numeric-literal-2} \end{array} \right\}$$

[GIVING data-name-3] [ROUNDED] [SIZE-ERROR-clause]

The BY-form signifies that the first operand (data-name 1 or numeric-literal-1) is the dividend (numerator), and the second operand (data-name-2 or numeric-literal-2) is the divisor (denominator). If GIVING is not written in this case, then the first operand must be a data-name in which the quotient is stored.

The INTO-form signifies that the first operand is the divisor and the second operand is the dividend. If GIVING is not written in this case, then the second operand must be a data-name in which the quotient is stored.

Use of the COMPUTE statement in preference to DIVIDE is recommended owing to the awkward syntax of the DIVIDE statement. Division by zero always causes a size-error condition.

6.15-8 COMPUTE Statement

The COMPUTE statement evaluates an arithmetic expression and then stores the result in a designated numeric or report item.

The format of the COMPUTE statement is:

COMPUTE data-name-1 [ROUNDED] =

$$\left\{ \begin{array}{l} \text{data-name-2} \\ \text{numeric-literal} \\ \text{arithmetic-expression} \end{array} \right\} \quad \text{[SIZE-ERROR-clause]}$$

An example of such a statement is:

COMPUTE GROSS-PAY ROUNDED = BASE-SALARY *

(1 + 1.5 * (HOURS − 40) / 40).

An arithmetic expression is a proper combination of numeric literals, data-names, arithmetic operators, and parentheses. In general, the data-names in an arithmetic expression must designate numeric data. Consecutive data-names (or literals) must be separated by an arithmetic operator, and *there must be one or more blanks on either side of the operator*. The operators are:

+   for addition
−   for subtraction
*   for multiplication
/   for division
** for exponentiation

Parenthesization may be specified when the normal order of operations is not desired. Consider the following expression.

$$A + B / (C - D * E)$$

Evaluation of the above expression is performed in the following ordered sequence:

1. Compute the product D times E, considered as intermediate result R1.
2. Compute intermediate result R2 as the difference C − R1.
3. Divide B by R2, providing intermediate result R3.
4. The final result is computed by addition of A to R3.

Without parentheses, the expression

$$A + B / C - D * E$$

is evaluated as:

R1 = B / C
R2 = A + R1
R3 = D * E
final result = R2 − R3

When parentheses are employed, the following punctuation rules are in effect.

1. A left parenthesis must be preceded by one or more spaces.
2. A right parenthesis must be followed by one or more spaces.

6.16 GO TO Statement

The GO TO statement permits the user to direct that the next statement to be executed is at the beginning of a specified procedure. Two forms of the GO TO statement are available in COBOL:

Option 1

GO TO procedure-name

Option 2

GO TO procedure-name . . . DEPENDING ON data-name

In Option 1 (simple GO TO), execution of the statement causes program control to be transferred to the designated procedure (either a paragraph or section). In Option 2, there are one or more procedures listed following the reserved words GO TO. Assuming there are n procedure-names, the statement represents an n-way "branch;" if the value of data-name is m, and m is in the range 1 to n, then execution is, in effect, a GO TO statement using the mth procedure-name listed in the statement. On the other hand, if m is not in the range 1-n, then the GO TO ... DEPENDING statement is inoperative, and the next statement in the normal sequence of program execution is taken. In an Option 2 GO TO statement, data-name must be that of a numeric field containing only integers (hence an embedded V in its Picture is prohibited).

6.17 IF Statement

The form of an IF statement is:

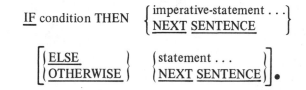

The condition may be:

1. A level 88 condition-name test (see Chapter 8)
2. A relation test
3. A sign test
4. A class test
5. A compound condition, which is a logical relationship between a combination of any of the simple test conditions listed in 1-4 above

When the condition is evaluated, the imperative statement(s) immediately following the condition are executed, if the condition is true, unless NEXT SENTENCE is written instead of imperative statements, in which case the next sentence is executed. If the evaluated condition is false, then the statement(s) after ELSE (or OTHERWISE) are executed, if any. In particular, this part of an IF statement may contain another IF.

Example 1   IF YEAR LESS THAN 1960 GO TO PREVIOUS-DECADE.

<u>Example 2</u>   IF YEAR LESS THAN 1960 MOVE DAY TO DAG, MOVE
MONTH TO MANAD, MOVE YEAR TO AR, ELSE MOVE
ZERO TO MANAD, DAG, AR.

<u>Example 3</u>   IF X = Y ADD 1 TO N, GO TO POINT-1, ELSE IF X > Y
GO TO POINT-2, ELSE GO TO POINT-3.

The following examples are invalid, for the reasons shown.

<u>Invalid Statement</u>	<u>Invalid Because:</u>
IF X = Y GO TO A, MOVE Y TO Z.	The Move statement will never be executed.
IF X = Y IF W = Z GO TO A, ELSE STOP RUN.	Condition must be followed by imperative statements (nested IF not recommended).

The relation test, sign test, class test, and compound conditions are defined and described in sections 6.17-1 through 6.17-4. The rules for comparisons are given in 6.17-5 and 6.17-6. Consideration of condition-name tests is taken up in Chapter 8, along with other advanced facilities of the COBOL language.

6.17-1   Relation Test

A simple relation test involves a subject, a relation, and an object. The subject is compared to the object to determine if the specified relation is true or false. For example, one may write:

IF NATIONALITY-CODE = 'C' GO TO P36.

The permissible relations are:

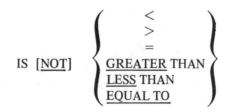

Either subject or object may be one of the following:

1. data-name
2. arithmetic expression (see 6.15-8).

3. figurative-constant

4. literal

Regardless of whether the reserved word or algebraic character relations are used, the normal COBOL punctuation is required, namely space(s) before and after the relation. The methods of evaluating comparisons are presented in 6.17-5 and 6.17-6.

6.17-2 Sign Test

The format of the sign test is:

$$
\left\{ \begin{array}{l} \text{data-name} \\ \text{arithmetic-expression} \end{array} \right\} \quad \text{IS [\underline{NOT}]} \quad \left\{ \begin{array}{l} \underline{\text{POSITIVE}} \\ \underline{\text{ZERO}} \\ \underline{\text{NEGATIVE}} \end{array} \right\}
$$

The subject (data-name or arithmetic expression) is tested to determine whether the object state (positive, negative, or zero) is true or false. The value zero is considered neither positive nor negative.

6.17-3 Class Test

The format of the class test is:

$$
\text{data-name IS [NOT]} \quad \left\{ \begin{array}{l} \underline{\text{NUMERIC}} \\ \underline{\text{ALPHABETIC}} \end{array} \right\}
$$

A character string item may be tested for either the numeric state or the alphabetic state; an external decimal item may be tested for the numeric state only (this is a form of error-checking). Regardless of the result of this test for a character string data item (defined by Picture X(n)), only numeric data-names are permitted in arithmetic expressions or other numeric contexts; the REDEFINES clause provides the means of defining both character string and external decimal attributes for a given data area.

6.17-4 Compound Conditions

Simple test-conditions can be combined with logical operators according to specified rules to form compound conditions. The logical operators are AND,

OR, and NOT. Two or more simple conditions combined by AND and/or OR make up a compound condition. The word OR is used to mean *either* or *both*. Thus, the expression A OR B is true if: A is true, or B is true, or both A and B are true. The word AND is used to mean both. Thus, the expression A AND B is true only if both A and B are true. The word NOT reverses the meaning of a relational operator. Thus, the expression NOT (A OR B) is true if A and B are false; and the expression NOT (A AND B) is true if A is false, B is false, or if both A and B are false. The logical operators and truth values are shown in Figure 6-6, where A and B represent simple conditions.

Condition		Related Conditions				
A	B	NOT A	A AND B	A OR B	NOT (A AND B)	NOT (A OR B)
True	True	False	True	True	False	False
False	True	True	False	True	True	False
True	False	False	False	True	True	False
False	False	True	False	False	True	True

Figure 6-6   Truth table (compound conditions).

Parentheses, which must always be paired, may be used to specify the order in which conditions are evaluated. Logical evaluation begins with the innermost pair of parentheses and proceeds to the outermost. If the order of evaluation is not specified by parentheses, the expression is evaluated in the following way:

1. Going from left to right, AND and its surrounding conditions are evaluated first.
2. Also working from left to right, OR and its surrounding conditions are then evaluated.

For example, the expression: A IS GREATER THAN B OR A IS EQUAL TO C AND D IS POSITIVE would be evaluated as if it were parenthesized as follows:

(A IS GREATER THAN B) OR ((A IS EQUAL TO C) AND
(D IS POSITIVE))

In most compilers (but not in some which operate in small computers), compound conditions may be written in an abbreviated form, in which the subject, or both the subject and relation, are implied. Examples are:

1. IF ITEM IS NUMERIC AND = 6, THEN GO TO SPECIAL-CASE.
2. IF TEMP = 6 OR 12 OR 18 OR < 0 GO TO LOCAL-DISTRIBUTION.

In example 1, the data-name ITEM-6 is the subject of the second relation (=6); in effect, the compiler remembers this data-name and inserts it between the word AND and the equal sign. In example 2, the programmer has properly omitted repetitions of "TEMP =", which the compiler remembers to insert after each appearance of the word OR, except the last, where only the name TEMP is inserted.

6.17-5 Numeric Comparisons

For numeric items, a relation test determines that the value of the subject is less than, equal to, or greater than the value of the object, regardless of the length. Numeric items are compared algebraically after alignment of decimal points.

6.17-6 Non-numeric Comparisons

For non-numeric items, a comparison results in the determination that one of the items is less than, equal to, or greater than the other, with respect to the collating sequence of characters. If the non-numeric items are of the same length, the comparison proceeds by comparing characters in corresponding character positions, starting from the left and continuing until either a pair of unequal characters or the last positions of each item are compared. The first pair of unequal characters encountered is compared for relative position in the collating sequence. The item containing the character that is positioned higher in the collating sequence is the greater item. The items are considered equal if all corresponding characters are equal. If the non-numeric items are of unequal length, comparison proceeds as described for items of the same length. If this process exhausts the characters of the shorter item, the shorter item is less than the longer unless the remainder of the longer item consists solely of spaces, in which case the items are equal.

Figure 6-7 depicts permissible comparisons between items of various types, and the mode of each comparison. Invalid comparisons are shown as blanks in the chart; numeric comparisons are shown as N; character-type comparisons are indicated by C.

First Operand	Second Operand					
	G	S	E	I	B	R
Group (G)	C	C	C	C	C	C
Character String (S)	C	C				C
External Decimal (E)	C		N	N	N	
Internal Decimal (I)	C		N	N	N	
Binary (B)	C		N	N	N	
Report (R)	C	C				C

Figure 6-7 Modes of comparison.

6.18 PERFORM Statement

The formats of the PERFORM statement are:

Option 1

$$\underline{\text{PERFORM}} \text{ range } \left[\begin{matrix} \begin{Bmatrix} \text{integer} \\ \text{data-name} \end{Bmatrix} \underline{\text{TIMES}} \\ \underline{\text{UNTIL}} \text{ condition} \end{matrix} \right]$$

Option 2

PERFORM	range VARYING data-name-1
FROM	initial-1 BY increment-1
UNTIL	condition-1 [AFTER data-name-2
FROM	initial-2 BY increment-2
UNTIL	condition-2] [AFTER data-name-3
FROM	initial-3 BY increment-3
UNTIL	condition-3]

In the above formats, the following definitions[8] apply:

range::= procedure-name-1 [THRU procedure-name-2]

---

[8] The notational symbol ::= means "is defined as".

$$initial::= \left\{ \begin{matrix} \text{data-name} \\ \text{numeric-literal} \end{matrix} \right\}$$

$$increment::= \left\{ \begin{matrix} \text{data-name} \\ \text{numeric-literal} \end{matrix} \right\}$$

The range specifies a contiguous body of procedural statements to be executed as a whole. Procedure-names designated in a range may be either paragraph-names or section-names.

Procedure-name-1 designates the starting point. If procedure-name-1 is a paragraph-name and procedure-name-2 is not given explicitly, then the range includes the entire paragraph. If procedure-name-2 is omitted and procedure-name-1 is a section-name, then the range includes the section in its entirety. If procedure-name-2 is present in the range specification, then the range includes all statements in procedure-name-2; consequently, if procedure-name-2 is a section, all its component paragraphs are executed before returning from the range. If procedure-name-2 is a paragraph-name, then the return point from the range is immediately after the last statement in the paragraph. In a range that is Performed, all paths must eventually lead to the terminal point of the range. The EXIT statement is provided as a means of defining a common terminal point to which all conditional paths of flow within a range lead. At any point in time, the active ranges being Performed must not coincide. It is not proper for multiple active ranges to share a common terminal point. However, it is proper for one range to be fully contained in another. See the illustration in Figure 6-9 for a depiction of legal and illegal ranges. When an exit is reached during the time it is the terminal point of an active Perform, the range is de-activated. In general, the time sequence of exits from active ranges must be in the inverse order of their activation. The identical range of a Perform must not be activated again while the range is active.

When a Performable range is *not* active, the sequence of statements is a natural one; that is, there is no implied return point at the end of the range. Hence such an inactive range may be executed in an "in-line fashion," and in this case the sequence of control "drops through" the last statement of a Performable range, continuing serially with the next statement (which is immediately *after* the range).

Whenever a PERFORM statement contains a condition (UNTIL), this condition is tested prior to activating (and executing) the range. If the condition is false, the range is executed; otherwise, the range is not executed. This may result in no executions of the range (if the condition is true at the outset).

Option 2 permits the programmer to vary one, two or three data-names (indexes)[9] in an orderly fashion. When two indexes are varied, the first index (data-name-1) is initialized to the value designated in the first FROM component of the statement. Assuming that condition-1 is false (the normal case), then the second index (data-name-2) is initialized as initial-2 (either a literal or data-name). Now condition-2 is tested; if false, as is usually the case at the outset, then the range is performed. Upon return, data-name-2 is incremented by the value increment-2, and condition-2 is tested. As long as condition-2 remains false, the range is executed repeatedly—and data-name-2 is incremented regularly while data-name-1 remains temporarily constant. Eventually condition-2 becomes true (for example, the condition may test whether data-name-2 has reached an upper limit)—at which point data-name-1 is incremented. If condition-1 is false, then the complete cycle of variations on data-name-2, again starting from initial-2, is repeated. By continuing in this way, data-name-1 is varied, and, within each step for data-name-1, data-name-2 undergoes a complete variation. The total PERFORM statement execution ceases only when condition-1 is true. An example of a PERFORM statement is:

PERFORM SET-ENTRY VARYING I FROM 1 BY 1 UNTIL I GREATER THAN I-MAX AFTER J FROM 1 BY 1 UNTIL J = J-MAX + 1.

An Option 2 Perform statement varying three indexes executes in a fashion similar to that described for the two-index case discussed above, except for the addition of one extra level of depth in the variation scheme.

Examples:

PERFORM INITIALIZATION.

PERFORM INPUT-VALIDATION THRU INPUT-VALIDATION-END TALLY TIMES.

PERFORM ITERATION UNTIL NEW-TERM LESS THAN 0.00001 OR NUMBER-OF-TERMS = 99.

Figure 6-8 illustrates, in the form of a flow chart, the logical steps involved in a PERFORM statement which varies three indexes. Figure 6-9 illustrates the permissible and invalid relationships between concurrently active PERFORM ranges.

---

[9] An index may be a subscript, but is not limited to being only a subscript.

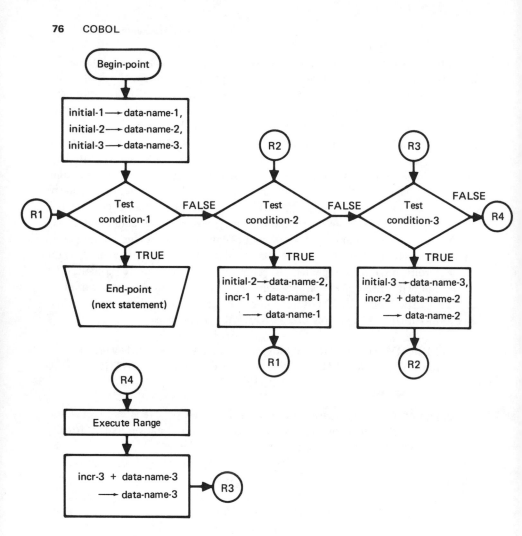

Figure 6-8   Logic of PERFORM varying 3 indexes.

6.19   EXIT Statement

The EXIT statement is used where it is necessary to provide an end point for a procedure.

The format for the EXIT statement is:

paragraph-name.   <u>EXIT</u>.

EXIT must appear in the source program as a one-word paragraph preceded by a paragraph-name. When the PERFORM statement is used, an EXIT paragraph-

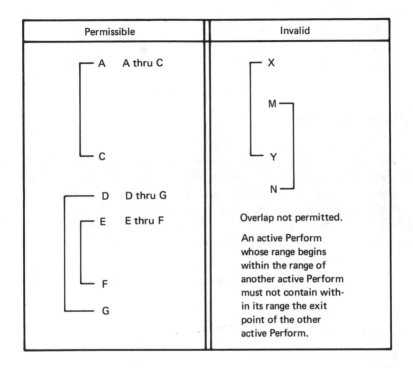

Permissible	Invalid

Figure 6-9 PERFORM ranges active concurrently.

name may be the procedure-name given as the operand in the THRU option. In this case, a statement in the range of an active PERFORM may transfer to an EXIT paragraph, bypassing the remainder of the statements in the range. In all other cases, EXIT paragraphs have no function and control passes sequentially through them to the first sentence of the next paragraph.

6.20 STOP Statement

The STOP statement is used to terminate or delay execution of the object program. The format of this statement is:

STOP RUN terminates execution of a program and returns control to the operating system. The form STOP literal causes a system-generated message code and the specified literal to be displayed on the console, and execution to be suspended. Execution of the program is resumed only after operator intervention: the specific intervention required is keying-in the aforementioned message code. Prior to responding in this way, the operator presumably performs a function suggested by the content of the literal.

6.21 Chapter Sign-off

You have learned a great deal about COBOL by now, including the basic Procedure Statements, and are now ready to do some serious programming.

Before you embark on that assignment, you should be aware that there are many COBOL features not explained so far in this book. Some of these matters are still to be considered, and others are not considered in great detail. Here are two lists which indicate how much more there is to learn:

Topics Considered Later in This Book

Qualification of Names
Condition-names (level 88)
CORRESPONDING Data-names
ALTER Statement
NOTE Statement
CONSTANT SECTION
TRANSFORM Statement
Declaratives and USE Sentences
ENTER and the LINKAGE SECTION
Sort Feature: SORT, RELEASE, and RETURN Statements
Debugging-Oriented Statements

Topics Excluded from This Book

Report Writer Feature
COPY and INCLUDE Statements

Exercises

1. Why must an OPEN statement be executed for a file prior to reading from it?

2. Find several alternative ways to express (in COBOL) the requirement to "go to the procedure named ERRONEOUS if the value of X is other than 1."

3. List which statements are imperative and explain where only imperative statements should appear.

4. The normal way for a program to cease execution is to execute the _____ statement.

5. Explain the errors in syntax.

    a. OPEN REVERSED INPUT FILE-1.

    b. READ FROM FILE-1.

    c. ADD X AND Y.

    d. WRITE OUTPUT AFTER ADVANCING 0 LINES.

    e. CLOSE FILE-7 WITHOUT LOCK.

    f. MOVE A, B TO C.

6. Write a program to balance your checking account. Card input data will represent the previous balance, each check or other debit, and deposits. How will a given input card's function (debit or credit) be determined? Output should be a printed listing of all detail input as well as the new balance.

7. In the following Working-storage table, total counts of transactions by type and by locality have been developed and stored where there are 8 transaction types and 15 different localities.

    01 SUMMARY-TABLE.

        02 BY-LOCALITY OCCURS 15.

          03 BY-TYPE OCCURS 8, COMPUTATIONAL.

            04 COUNT PICTURE S9(7).

Write the necessary additional Working-storage and Procedural Statements to form

    a. Totals for each type, regardless of locality.

    b. Totals for each locality, regardless of type.

    c. One grand total.

8. Input in a numeric field may range from one to five digits; numbers of less than 5 digits are input with leading blanks (e.g., blank blank 3 4 7).

Write Data and Procedural Statements to transform leading blanks to zero and then require that the field be numeric. Non-numeric data shall be rejected (GO TO REJECT); valid data shall permit further processing.

9. Write a COBOL program which outputs a data deck that is the mirror image of the input data deck. That is, each output card

corresponds to an input card, except that data formerly in column 1 appears in column 80; data formerly in column 2 appears in column 79, etc.

10. Write an internal sort program. Input is alphanumeric data in card columns 2-61; output is the same data reordered on the basis of the computer's inherent collating sequence. You may assume a fixed maximum number of cards to be input, but the program must be able to function with a lesser number of inputs (including none!). What will your program do if more than the maximum data cards are supplied as input? Output should be a print-out of the sorted character strings.

11. Write a self-duplicating program, i.e. one which punches a source program identical to itself, card for card and character for character on each card. The program is to have no input files.

12. Depreciation accounting has as its purpose the systematic distribution of cost (or other basis of value) of tangible capital assets over the estimated life of an entity.

The depreciation rate is applied to the cost of the asset in the first year. In successive years, the depreciation rate is applied to the declining book value (i.e., to the cost minus accumulated depreciation).

Use the following data names:

COST is the original cost of the subject asset.

BOOK (i) is the book value at the end of year i.

DEPRECIATION (i) is the amount of depreciation charged during year i.

ACCELERATION-FACTOR is a factor, limited by law not to exceed 2.0, which is a multiple of the straight-line method.

YEARS is the life of the asset.

In year $i = 1$, depreciation is computed as the product of acceleration times cost, divided by the *fixed* life of the asset (in years). The difference of cost minus depreciation then determines book value at end of year 1.

Thenceforth, the process is carried out for the number of years specified, using the previous book value instead of cost.

Write a COBOL program which will accept COST ($\leqslant$ $999,999.99), YEARS ($\leqslant$ 99), and ACCELERATION-FACTOR ($\leqslant$ 2.00) from one card and produce a table of depreciations and book value for each year specified. After one table has been produced, the program should recycle for more data, ending only when there are no more input cards.

7

WRITING A COBOL FILE
MAINTENANCE PROGRAM

7.1 Program Requirements

A program (named TAPEUPD) to maintain a master file on tape is required. The data records are 80 characters long. The first 75 characters consist of information (it could be a program file or a data file); the last five characters contain a record number created by the program. Using the record numbers, it may be necessary to do either of the following (or both) at some later time:

1. Delete certain records
2. Insert new records at specified points in the file.

Therefore our program must be able to

1. Create the file from cards and assign record numbers at the same time.
2. Update the file. Traditionally and for very sound reasons of file security, updating of tape files is done by copying the "old" master file onto a new reel of tape, except as modified by the transactions which cause some old records to be deleted or new records to be created. At the completion of an update run, the output tape is saved as the current master file. The old master is saved, too, for back-up purposes.

7.2 Input Specifications for TAPEUPD

The first data card shall be construed as an option card. If it contains the data 'ORIGINATE' in columns 1-9, the program run shall create the file. There will be no old master file in this case. If the option card contains the data 'UPDATE' in columns 1-6, the program run will be an update run. In an UPDATE run, there are three possible subsequent card inputs:

1. Columns 1-6 contain 'INSERT'
2. Columns 1-6 contain 'DELETE'
3. All other cases.

In an ORIGINATE run, all input cards subsequent to the option card are treated simply as data (columns 1-75) to be placed on tape. INSERT and DELETE cards must have a five-digit number in columns 10-14; a DELETE card may have another fixed-digit number in columns 16-20. The five-digit number on an INSERT card refers to the record of the old master file beyond which a new record will be placed during the overall tape-copy operation. The data (one or more data cards) to be inserted immediately follows the INSERT card.

A DELETE card which is blank in columns 16-20 is treated as if the same number appearing in columns 10-14 also were in columns 16-20. The two five-digit numbers in a DELETE card (the second one must not be less than the first one) designate a range of records which are to be excluded from the tape-copying operation.

In an UPDATE run, the changes to the file must be in order. Thus, all the record numbers in a change deck (in either INSERT or DELETE cards) must constitute a monotonically ascending series.

7.3 Flowcharting

One of the most powerful tools available to computer programming personnel is the flowchart. A flowchart is a logical diagram showing the ordered sequence of program actions and decisions. A few simple conventions are employed in order to standardize the flowchart and thus make it understandable not only to the immediately involved programmer, but to his management as well. Because the flowchart is highly regarded as a key piece of documentation associated with a program, it is a necessity even if the programmer does not need it as a planning aid for the programming chore.

A flowchart should convey the functional nature of each program part in terms of the external requirements. A common error in making a flowchart is simply to enclose the program statements themselves in the various shapes of a flowchart. A good flowchart relates to the intent of the programmer, not to the programming language techniques used in accomplishing the end goal.

In a flowchart, a rectangular shape encloses a functional description which is an unconditional step in the overall process. Only one line, connecting to another point of the flowchart, emanates from a function box.

One common notational convention is to use an arrow meaning "is moved into," within a rectangular function box. For example,

means "move the value 4 into the field named TEMP."

A conditional step (a test or decision) is drawn as a rhombus shape and has two or more lines emanating from it; each line bears a notation of the condition under which that particular path is taken. Example:

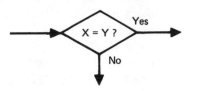

The case of end-of-file detection in the attempted reading of a file is indicated by the letters eof; in this instance, one line emanating from the function box is labeled "eof," and the other is unlabeled, representing the non-eof (normal) case.

In a decision rhombus, the colon (:) symbol placed between two quantities means that a comparison is to be made; the lines coming from the rhombus may be labeled $=$ $<$ $>$ $\geqslant$ $\leqslant$ $\neq$ for equal, less than, greater than, greater than or equal to, less than or equal to, or not equal to, respectively.

Each key point of a flowchart (normally corresponding to a procedure-name) is labeled by enclosing the procedure-name in a circle or oval and connecting this to a decision rhombus or function box. When a program step leads to another part of the program, this is shown by drawing a line to a circle in which the requisite procedure-name is placed Figure 7-1 illustrates these two usages; the leftmost oval (Start) is a procedure-name point of definition, and the rightmost circle is a reference to a procedure elsewhere in the flowchart.

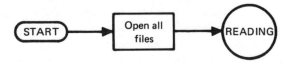

Figure 7-1 Illustration of procedure-name
definition and reference.

7.4 Flowchart of TAPEUPD

In the flowchart appearing on pages 85-89, which is a design document from which the COBOL program may be written, we employ a useful convention; when we desire to PERFORM a well defined procedure elsewhere in the program, we will simply place the name of that procedure, in capital letters, in a function box. In the flowchart of TAPEUPD, the following notation is used:

SWITCH   ...   a data field having value 0, 1, 2, or 3 depending on what type of card is read by the READ-CARD section.

R1   ...   a field in Working-Storage which contains the reference number from the most recent INSERT or DELETE card.

R2   ...   a field in Working-Storage which contains the second reference number of a DELETE card.

CD-EOF   ...   a data field, initially containing SPACE, which indicates that the end of the card file has not yet been encountered. Change to 'A' when card file eof is detected.

Appendix C contains a listing of TAPEUPD as programmed for the IBM System 360 Disk Operating System (DOS) COBOL. The program as shown is checked out and has been used extensively in the "production" mode.

Exercises

1. Write a program capable of performing a "selective" file copy. Input are three numeric quantities $m, n,$ and p. Output shall be copied from a given file by repeating the following sequence of steps p times:
   Step a ... skip m records
   Step b ... copy the next n records.
2. What will happen to your selective file copy program if m, or n, or p is input as a negative or zero or non-numeric value? Analyze each possibility. How can your program be improved to avoid malfunction due to bad input?
3. Develop a COBOL program to perform some useful practical task, such as an interest-compounding printout. Development should begin with a written statement of the problem, then a flowchart, which is evaluated "by hand" for sample data. Finally, after you are assured that the method is correct, you may do the COBOL coding.

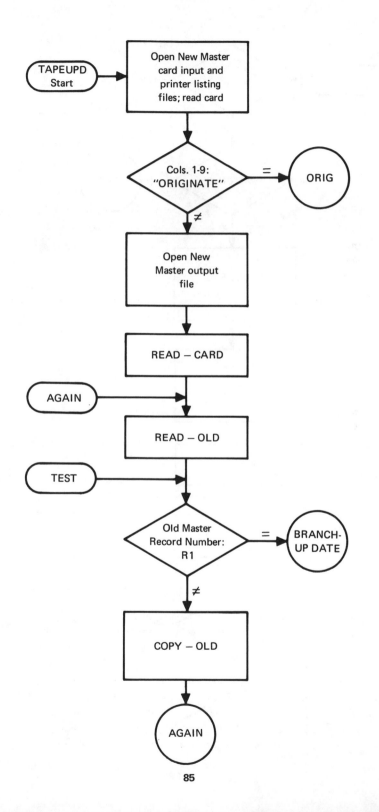

85

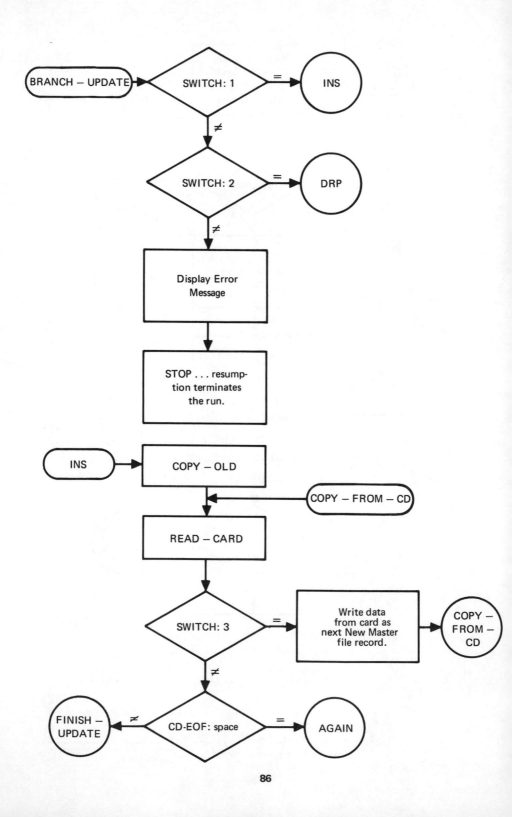

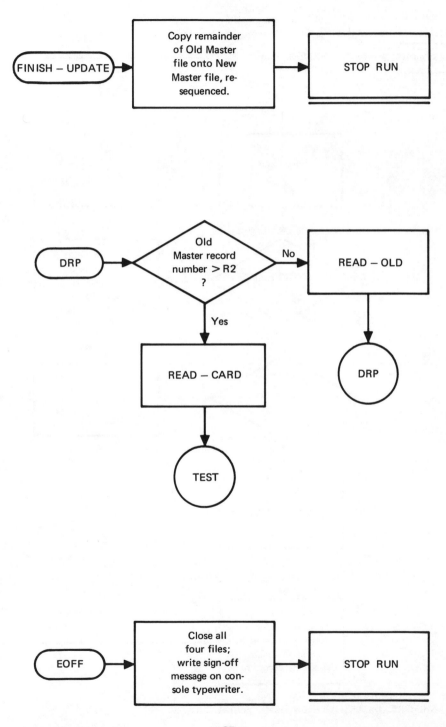

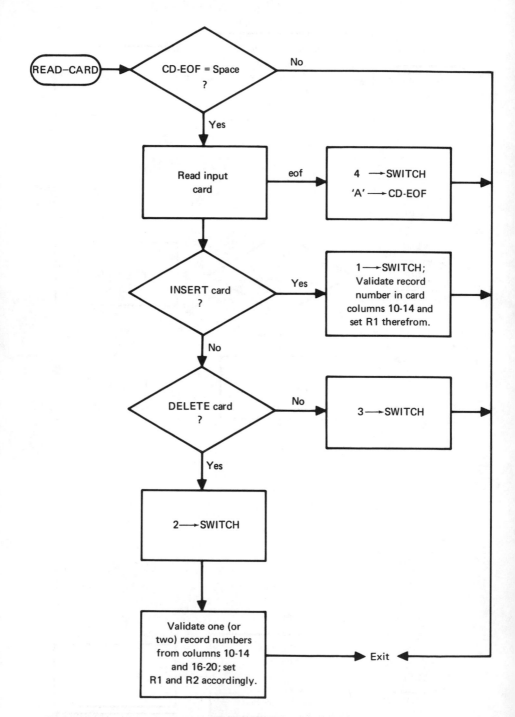

Note: READ-CARD is a self-contained performable section.

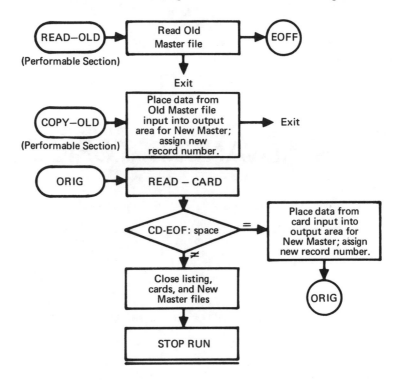

4. The input to a simple payroll program is one card per employee, as follows:

Card columns	Content
1 - 6	employee number
7 - 26	name
27 - 30	pay rate ($$.¢¢) per hour
32 - 34	hours worked (XX.X)
35	department number

Write a program to compute take-home pay = gross − deductions, where gross = pay rate × hours worked if the latter does not exceed 40.0. For those hours above 40.0 per week, the payrate is increased by 50% ("time-and-a-half"). Define a graduated tax table for withholding based on gross. What should the printed outputs in the report be?

5. Augment your program for Exercise 4 by incorporating a capability for accumulation of up to nine different department subtotals of hours, gross, and take-home pay. Do not assume that input data is in order by department. (This exercise should be done using subscripts.)

8

ADVANCED TOPICS

In this chapter, we present a number of COBOL features that may be considered advanced in nature.

8.1 Qualification of Names

Every name used in a COBOL source program must be unique within the source program in either of two ways:

1. Because no other name has the identical spelling.
2. Because the name exists within a hierarchy of names, so that the name can be made unique by mentioning one or more of the higher levels of the hierarchy. The higher levels are called qualifiers when this method of insuring uniqueness is used. The process is called qualification. (Warning: Higher levels have numerically smaller level numbers.)

The following rules apply to the qualification of names:

1. The word OF or IN must precede each qualifying name, and the names must appear in ascending order of hierarchy.
2. A qualifier must be of a higher level and within the same hierarchy as the name it is qualifying.

3. The same name must not appear at two levels in a hierarchy in such a manner that it would appear to qualify itself.
4. The highest level qualifier must be unique. Each qualifying name must be unique at its own level within the hierarchy of the immediately higher qualifier.
5. Qualification when not needed is permitted.

These rules apply to qualification of data-names, condition names, and procedure-names. For File Section data-names, the highest level qualifier is the file-name. For other data-names, the highest qualificater is the appropriate level 01 group name. For condition-names, qualification is by name of the previous elementary item, and its qualifiers in turn if necessary. Qualification of a procedural paragraph-name by a section-name is permitted. Any combination of qualifiers that will insure uniqueness may be used. For example, using Figure 4-1 and the data hierarchy in section 4.2, we may write the following qualified name references.

NAME-OF-EMPLOYEE IN PAYROLL-RECORD
MM OF HIRE-DATE
DD OF PAYROLL-RECORD.

The key word FILLER may not be used as a qualifier.

A data-name cannot be subscripted when it is used as a qualifier; however, the entire qualified data-name may be subscripted. Referring to Figure 5-4, we note that the following name references in which the qualifier is stated prior to the subscript, are permissible.

ELEMENT OF ARRAY (I).
ELEMENT IN ARRAY (2).

8.2 Condition-names

The general form of a condition-name entry is:

88 condition-name VALUE IS literal

A condition-name is a name given to a possible value that may be assumed by a data item and is formed according to the rules for data-name formation. A level 88 entry must be preceded either by another level 88 entry (in the case of several consecutive condition-names pertaining to an elementary item) or by an elementary item. Every condition-name pertains to an elementary item in such a way that the condition-name may be qualified by the name of the elementary item and the elementary item's qualifiers. A condition-name is used in the Procedure Division in place of a simple relational condition. A condition-name may pertain to an elementary item (a conditional variable) requiring subscripts. In this case, the condition-name, when written in the Procedure Division, must be subscripted according to the same requirements as the associated elementary item. The type of literal in a condition-name entry must be consistent with the data type of the conditional variable. In the following example, PAYROLL-PERIOD is the conditional variable. The picture associated with it limits the value of the 88 condition-name to one digit.

```
02 PAYROLL-PERIOD PICTURE IS 9.
    88 WEEKLY VALUE IS 1.
    88 SEMI-MONTHLY VALUE IS 2.
    88 MONTHLY VALUE IS 3.
```

Using the above description, one may write the procedural condition-name test:

IF MONTHLY GO TO DO-MONTHLY.

An equivalent statement is:

IF PAYROLL-PERIOD = 3 GO TO DO-MONTHLY.

An equivalent example (using qualification) is:

IF MONTHLY IN PAYROLL-PERIOD GO TO DO-MONTHLY.

8.3 CORRESPONDING Data-names

This feature, highly regarded by some, is one of the most complicated parts of COBOL. Because of its complexity, it can be dangerous in the hands of the inexperienced and is not recommended to the typical user. Because of its characteristic of accomplishing so much as a result of such little direction from the user, many critics warn experts to avoid the CORRESPONDING feature.

The CORRESPONDING feature is available in MOVE, ADD, or SUBTRACT statements. The appropriate statement forms are:

MOVE CORRESPONDING data-name-1 TO data-name-2

ADD CORRESPONDING data-name-1
TO data-name-2   [ROUNDED]   [SIZE-ERROR-clause]

SUBTRACT CORRESPONDING data-name-1 FROM
data-name-2   [ROUNDED]   [SIZE-ERROR-clause]

If rules 1–5 below are satisfied, two items subordinate to the group items data-name-1 and data-name-2 are CORRESPONDING items.

1. Items are CORRESPONDING data items if the respective data-names are the same, including all qualification up to but not including data-name-1 and data-name-2.
2. Data-name-1 and data-name-2 must be group items.
3. Of the items subordinate to data-name-1 or data-name-2 the following are not considered CORRESPONDING items:
   a. An item named by the key word FILLER and any items subordinate to it.
   b. An item described by a REDEFINES or OCCURS clause, and any items subordinate to it.

   However, the items designated by data-name-1 and data-name-2 may be described with REDEFINES or OCCURS clauses, or be subordinate to other group items whose descriptions have REDEFINES or OCCURS clauses.
4. If either data-name-1 or data-name-2 is described with an OCCURS clause, it must be subscripted; each data item that corresponds will be subscripted by the compiler.
5. In determining which are corresponding data items, only the first complete description of any area will be considered in the case where a REDEFINES clause has been used. Consider the following data organization:

   01 A
   02 B
   02 C   REDEFINES B
   03 D
   03 E
   02 F

   Only B or F can be considered as potential corresponding items.

In ADD or SUBTRACT statements having the CORRESPONDING option only corresponding numeric items are selected. In MOVE CORRESPONDING, only one of the fields in each selected pair need be elementary. Thus, any time CORRESPONDING is used, the effect is the same as if a series of ADD, SUBTRACT, or MOVE statements had been written.

8.4 ALTER Statement

The ALTER statement format is:

ALTER   { paragraph-name-1 <u>TO PROCEED</u> <u>TO</u> procedure-name-2 }   . . .

The ALTER Statement is used to modify a simple GO TO statement elsewhere in the Procedure Division, thus changing the sequence in which program steps are executed.

Paragraph-name-1 must be a paragraph consisting only of a simple GO TO statement. The ALTER statement in effect replaces the former operand of that particular GO TO by procedure-name-2. Example:

```
GATE. GO TO OPEN-MASTER-FILE.
OPEN-MASTER-FILE.
    ALTER GATE TO PROCEED TO POINT-A.
    OPEN INPUT MASTER.
POINT-A.
    READ MASTER, AT END GO TO QUIT.
```

Program TAPEUPD (Appendix C) uses the ALTER statement (sequence number 000670).

8.5 NOTE Statement

The NOTE statement permits the programmer to write explanatory comments in the Procedure Division of a source program. The format of the NOTE statement is:

<u>NOTE</u> comment . . .

NOTE, when used, must begin a sentence. Following the word NOTE, any combination of words or literals may appear. If NOTE is not the first word in a paragraph, the comments end with a period followed by a space. If NOTE is the first word of a paragraph, any subsequent sentences within the paragraph structure must be observed. A Note sentence or paragraph is listed in the source program printout, but has no effect on the compilation.

8.6 Constant Section

In some compilers, the Data Division may include a Constant Section, which follows the Working-storage Section. The Constant Section is not implemented in IBM System 360, RCA Spectra 70, and XDS Sigma COBOL compilers; therefore named constants are included in the Working-Storage Section.

8.7 TRANSFORM Statement

In IBM System 360 and RCA Spectra 70 COBOL compilers, a TRANS-FORM statement (procedural) is available to permit characters to be mapped into specified alternates. The reader should consult the appropriate manufacturer's COBOL manual for detailed specifications.

8.8 Declaratives and USE Sentences

The content of Declaratives, facilities available, and restrictions imposed on these facilities are highly dependent on the design characteristics of individual computer operating systems. The USE Sentence may only appear immediately after a section-name definition within the Declaratives region. The Declaratives region, if present, must immediately follow the Procedure Division header. The region is defined by the appearance of the key word DECLARATIVES (followed by a period) in Margin A; the region is terminated by END DECLARATIVES. Within the Declaratives region, which must be arranged in sections, one writes procedures to be performed implicitly when the operating system detects the occurrence of certain special events, such as:

1. label creation on output.
2. label checking on input.
3. I/O error detection.

For each such possible event, there is a USE sentence, as explained in the following discussions. Declarative Sections dealing with labels are entered at the time of opening and/or closing a file. The general format of the Declaratives region is:

> PROCEDURE DIVISION.
> DECLARATIVES.
> ⎰ section-name SECTION. USE-sentence.⎱
> ⎱ {paragraph-name. sentence}   ⎰   ...
> END DECLARATIVES.

A declarative section or any of its paragraphs may not be referred to by any statement outside the section. The compiler generates a code at the end of each section in order to make the proper return to the operating system.

8.8-1   USE FOR CREATING LABELS (Output)

The format of the USE FOR CREATING LABELS (Output) sentence in the IBM 360 and RCA Spectra 70 is:

$$\underline{\text{USE}} \text{ FOR CREATING } \left[\begin{array}{c}\underline{\text{BEGINNING}} \\ \underline{\text{ENDING}}\end{array}\right] \underline{\text{LABELS}} \text{ ON}$$

$$\underline{\text{OUTPUT}} \text{ file-name } \ldots$$

When this statement appears for a given file-name, the associated Declarative Section is entered, under operating system control so that the user may process "user label" record(s).

The reader should consult the appropriate manufacturer's COBOL manual for detailed discussions of user labels and their handling. When neither the word BEGINNING nor ENDING appears in this USE sentence, the Declarative is executed for both user header and trailer-label writing.

8.8-2   USE FOR CHECKING LABELS (Input)

The format of the USE FOR CHECKING LABELS (Input) sentence in the IBM 360 and RCA Spectra 70 is:

$$\underline{\text{USE}} \text{ FOR CHECKING } \left[\begin{array}{c}\underline{\text{BEGINNING}} \\ \underline{\text{ENDING}}\end{array}\right] \underline{\text{LABELS}} \text{ ON}$$

$$\underline{\text{INPUT}} \text{ file-name } \ldots$$

When this statement identifies a Declarative Section, the section is entered to allow the user to validate or extract supplementary label information on certain INPUT or I-O files. Again, the reader is advised to consult the appropriate manufacturer's manual for further details.

8.8-3   File Error Declarative Section

The statement form <u>USE</u> <u>AFTER</u> STANDARD <u>ERROR</u> PROCEDURE ON file-name is provided in order to identify a Declarative section to be executed after the standard error-recovery attempts have been made by the operating system. Within any such section, the designated file may not be referred to by any statement except CLOSE. When the normal exit from the section is taken, the error is ignored and processing continues, if possible. For further detail, consult the appropriate manufacturer's COBOL manual.

8.9   Inter-module Communication (ENTER and LINKAGE Section)

Separately compiled COBOL program modules may be combined into a single executable program. Inter-module communication is made possible through the use of the LINKAGE Section of the Data Division (which follows the Working-Storage Section) and by executing special supplementary statements provided through the ENTER facility. In this section, we shall present details of inter-module communication as implemented in the IBM System 360 and RCA Spectra 70 COBOL compilers.

8.9-1   LINKAGE Section

This section describes data made available in memory from either another program module or User Label Record Areas. Record description entries in the LINKAGE section provide data-names by which data-areas reserved in memory by other programs may be referenced. Entries in the LINKAGE section do not reserve memory areas because the data is assumed to be present elsewhere in memory.

The LINKAGE section is required in any program module in which there appears a LABEL RECORDS clause with a data-name option or an ENTRY statement with a USING option. The LINKAGE section serves as a data-referencing mechanism between a program and the User Label record area or between a main (calling) program and its (called) subprogram. In the latter case, the LINKAGE section must be present in the called program. Any Record Description clause may be used to describe items in the LINKAGE Section as long as the following rules are adhered to:

1. The rules concerning contiguous and noncontiguous storage specified for the Working-storage section.
2. The VALUE clause may not be specified for other than level 88 items.
3. Level 01 items are assumed to start on a double-word boundary. It is the programmer's responsibility to ensure proper alignment between an argument (pointer to data) in a CALL statement and the corresponding data-name in an ENTRY statement. (See 8.9-2)
4. Data-names defined in the Linkage Section other than a User Label record area may not be referenced until the ENTRY statement containing the data-name has been activated.

8.9-2 ENTER Statement

The ENTER statement notifies the compiler that certain nonstandard COBOL statements follow:

1. A CALL statement, which transfers to an entry point in a separately compiled subprogram. Arguments (pointers to data) may be passed to the subprogram.
2. An ENTRY declaration, which defines a subprogram entry point. The definition may also list dummy data-names corresponding to passed arguments.
3. A RETURN statement, signifying the end of a subprogram and return to the calling program.

The ENTER statement has the following two formats:

Option 1 (Used in a calling program)

> ENTER LINKAGE
> CALL entry-name [USING argument] . . .
> ENTER COBOL.

Option 2 (Used in a COBOL subprogram)

> ENTER LINKAGE
> ENTRY entry-name [USING data-name] . . .
> ENTER COBOL.
>
> .
> .
> .
>
> COBOL statements
>
> .
> .
> .
>
> ENTER LINKAGE.   RETURN.   ENTER COBOL.

In option 1, entry-name is any alphanumeric combination of no more than 8 characters enclosed in quotation marks. The entry-name must be distinct from any other entry-name or program-name as given in the PROGRAM-ID paragraph.

In option 2, the data-names in the USING list must be level 01 or 77 LINKAGE Section items. In the USING clause of Option 1, an argument may be one of the following:

1. A data-name when calling a COBOL subprogram.
2. A data-name, file-name, or a procedure-name when calling a subprogram written in a language other than COBOL.

Option 2 is used to establish an entry point in a COBOL subprogram. Control is transferred to the entry point by a CALL statement in another program. *Entry-name* defines the entry point which establishes availability of the data arguments passed by the external CALL statement. Computer address pointers for data items in the USING list of an ENTRY statement are obtained from the USING list of the associated CALL statement. Items in the two USING lists (that of the CALL in the main program and that of the ENTRY in the subprogram) are paired in one-to-one correspondence. There is no necessary relationship between the actual names used for such paired items, but the data descriptions must be equivalent. When a group data item is named in the USING list of an ENTRY statement, names subordinate to it in the subprogram's Linkage Section may be employed in subsequent procedural statements. Because the compiler assumes that each LINKAGE record (level 01 or 77 entry) starts with the leftmost byte of a double word[10] the data items passed by a CALL must also adhere to the same restriction. The RETURN statement enables the return from a subprogram to the first instruction after the CALL statement in the calling program. There must be no path of program flow to an ENTRY statement within the program containing the ENTRY statement. Hence, the preceding ENTER LINKAGE statement should not have a paragraph name.

---

[10] A double word address is an exact multiple of 8, in terms of a byte-addressable memory.

9

DEBUGGING COBOL PROGRAMS

Programmers use the word "debug" as a verb meaning "eliminate program errors." The art of debugging is a critical one, and the skills required are difficult to quantify. Good debugging technique is based not only on knowledge and experience (which the beginner obviously does not possess), but also on inspiration and imagination (which every beginner should have). These latter abilities, which involve the ability to mentally play out a systematic process while checking the details of its implementation along the way, are instrumental in the detection of actual or potential program flaws. Coupled with proper analysis, the errors which occurred in a program run can be explained, and hence corrected. But the best debugging is not *post mortem* analysis, but proper care and caution in the design and coding stages of producing a computer program. (We have previously stressed the benefits of flowcharting in this regard.) One of the best aids to debugging is the compiler itself. Every compiler provides a summary of errors detected in the course of a compilation run; this error summary consists of "diagnostic" messages, usually printed in order by source-program line numbers. Analysis of these messages (if any) helps eliminate early program errors which may take the form of a keypunch error (mis-spelling), omission of required key words, or high-order truncation in a MOVE statement. Thus, the programmer usually has a high degree of confidence in his program when it finally compiles in error-free form.[11] Using test data prepared

[11] Some compilers have a propensity for issuing "warning" messages concerned with trivia such as bytes skipped between Working-storage records. These are generally simply ignored by the user.

with any degree of cleverness or laxity, the program is available to start executing at this point. Particularly in the more recent computers, bad data causes a program to "blow up" during execution if the program is naively constructed. Therefore, it is incumbent on every COBOL programmer to perform data validation (within the program) for two major reasons:

1. The properness of the data, in terms of what type of data is expected at any given time, must be assured.
2. The properness of the data, in the application context, must be validated.

As an illustration of our second reason above, we can point out that known real limits should be programmed into a computer job. For example, if it is known that the maximum hourly pay rate is $8.75, then our three-digit input field should not contain any number larger than 875. But our input field should not be blank or contain any letters, asterisks, or other improper characters. This illustrates our first, more general reason for requiring data validation. In short, if our program requires only numeric hourly rates as the basis for computations, and if the data preparation has not been previously checked (by computer), then our program must do the job. With this introduction to the concept of Plan Ahead alertness, let us now list a number of trouble-preventive recommendations.

9.1 Validation of Data

Numeric data in external decimal form (e.g., coming from cards) should always be checked for validity. Otherwise, a machine interruption[12] will occur, causing an abnormal end of job (with dump).

E.g., IF TYPE-FIELD NOT NUMERIC GO TO INVALID-TYPE-HANDLER, ELSE GO TO T1 T2 T3 T4 DEPENDING ON TYPE-FIELD.

9.2 Don't Get Fooled by Your Own Logic

It is very easy to foul up an IF statement and leave a logical loose end, creating an unexpected program flow path.

Consider the following example. The program requirement is to assure that the input card column in question contains only blank or any of the digits 0, 1, or 2. One programmer "solved" this requirement by the following coding:

[12]Data exception.

03 AMIL-CODE-NU   PICTURE 9.

03 MAIL-CODE REDEFINES MAIL-CODE-NU PICTURE X.

IF MAIL-CODE-NU NOT NUMERIC AND

MAIL-CODE NOT = SPACE OR

MAIL-CODE-NU GREATER THAN 2 GO TO MC-NG.

If a blank (SPACE) exists, then the NOT NUMERIC condition is true; the NOT = SPACE condition is therefore false. Then we have (true AND false) OR GREATER THAN 2.

False

Now, to determine truth value of the overall condition, the space in the field will be tested against 2. However, this is a violation of COBOL rules—a machine interrupt will occur (in the IBM 360, for example) in treating the space numerically for the last condition. Therefore this is an improper statement. Numerous simpler and safe solutions can be devised. One solution is:

IF MAIL-CODE-NU NUMERIC NEXT SENTENCE

ELSE IF MAIL-CODE NOT = SPACE

GO TO MC-NG. IF MAIL-CODE-NU>

2 GO TO MC-NG.

9.3   IF Punctuation Is Critical

In testing for which of several possible values may be in a given field, a series of IF statements may be used. However, it is very important that these be organized by proper punctuation in order to avoid an effect other than the one intended.

In the following, the code sequence is flawed because the program design permits only "R" or "B" as Run-Option values.

IF RUN-OPTION = 'R' MOVE 'REWORK-RUN' TO TITLE-AREA-3.

IF RUN-OPTION = 'B' MOVE 'INITIAL-BALANCING'

TO TITLE-AREA-3 ELSE STOP 'ERROR, RUN OPTION'.

The above code works well if "B" is the input data value; however, if "R" is the value, MOVE in the first sentence is executed and then the second IF is executed, where, because the data value is not "B", the ELSE branch of the second IF statement is executed resulting in a program stop accompanied by a printed message stating that the Run Option is erroneous. One remedy is to eliminate the first period and replace it with another ELSE. Can you recommend another way to code this properly?

9.4 PERFORM Ranges Can Be Tricky

Use of PERFORM is very advantageous. However, if one is careless, an unsuspected error may arise, as illustrated below.

A.   PERFORM TEST.
.
.
.
TEST. IF I = O GO TO END-TEST.

MOVE CHAR (I) TO FIELD (I).

END-TEST. EXIT.

The Perform at A sets up an exit *between* the last statement of paragraph TEST and the paragraph END-TEST. Therefore the case I = O causes control to pass *beyond* the return mechanism, and improper flow results. A possible correction is:

A.   PERFORM TEST THRU END-TEST.

Because of this complexity, it is recommended that the object of a PERFORM be a section whenever possible. In IBM System 360 COBOL, from the point where the first section begins, all subsequent code must be organized into sections. This means that all Performable code is concentrated at the end of the program for followers of this credo. In many other compilers, including the RCA Spectra 70 and XDS Sigma families, the entire Procedure Division must be organized into sections if there are any sections at all.

9.5 Semi-infinite Disaster Potential

Many other things can go wrong. A partial list includes:

1. Attempting to ACCEPT data from the card reader when there is no more data.

2. Mounting the wrong unlabeled file on a tape drive, so that a record input error of the wrong length results.

3. Executing a write statement which failed to have an AFTER ADVANCING suffix for a Printer file for which other WRITEs exist *with* the AFTER ADVANCING suffix.

4. Having a wrong control card set-up.

5. Failing to properly initialize data areas in Working-storage, which results in unpredictable starting values for counters, totals, etc.

6. Making reference to fields in files which are not in open status.

The point here is that none of the above errors is of a type detectable by the compiler, so an execution-time debugging facility is needed.

In the third generation COBOL compilers (System 360, Spectra 70, and Sigma series), three extremely valuable features oriented toward debugging were added: the READY TRACE, RESET TRACE, and EXHIBIT statements, which are the topics in the next two sections of this chapter.

9.6 Tracing a COBOL Execution

The execution TRACE mode may be set or reset dynamically. When set, procedure-names are printed in the order in which they are executed.

Execution of the READY TRACE statement sets the trace mode to cause printing of every section and paragraph name each time it is entered. The RESET TRACE statement inhibits such printing. Possession of a printed list of procedure-names in the order of their execution is invaluable in detection of a program malfunction; it aids in detection of the point at which actual program flow departed from the expected program flow. Another debugging feature may be required in order to reveal critical data values at specifically designated points in the procedure. The EXHIBIT statement provides this facility.

9.7 The EXHIBIT Statement

With this statement, the user can obtain a printout of data (a) whenever its value is observed to have changed and/or (b) in self-identified form. The basic format of the statement is:

$$\text{EXHIBIT} \left\{ \begin{array}{l} \underline{\text{NAMED}} \\ \underline{\text{CHANGED}} \ \underline{\text{NAMED}} \end{array} \right\} \left\{ \begin{array}{l} \text{data-name} \\ \text{nonnumeric-literal} \end{array} \right\} \ \ldots$$

Warning: In IBM DOS/360, each Exhibit statement must be a separate sentence (i.e., must be ended by period punctuation).

The execution of an EXHIBIT NAMED statement causes a display of the designated data or nonnumeric literal. The format of the output for each data-name listed in a NAMED or CHANGED NAMED form of an EXHIBIT statement is:

Blank

Original data-name (including qualifiers, if written)

Blank

Equal sign

Blank

Value of data-name

The CHANGED NAMED form of the Exhibit statement causes a printout of each changed value for items listed in the statement. Only those values representing changes and their identifying names are printed. The CHANGED form of the EXHIBIT statement provides for a display of items when they change value compared to the value at the previous time the EXHIBIT statement was executed. The first time such a statement is executed all values are considered changed; they are displayed and saved for purposes of comparison.

1. When two distinct EXHIBIT CHANGED statements appear in a program, changes in data-name are associated with the two separate statements. Depending on the path of program flow, the values of data-names saved for comparison may differ for the two statements.

2. When the list of operands in the EXHIBIT CHANGED statement includes literals, the literals are printed as remarks.

Literals listed in the EXHIBIT statement are preceded by a blank when displayed. The sum of the sizes of the operands in an EXHIBIT statement may not exceed the maximum logical record length of the system's logical output device. By using the debugging features now available in COBOL, the programmer has available the necessary tools to develop and check out COBOL programs in a fraction of the time and cost formerly required in COBOL and still required by users of assembly-level languages.

9.8 A Typical Debugging Diary

The RWLIST program (Appendix E) was developed on July 8, 1970 and run at the Xerox Data Systems plant in El Segundo, California on the following day.

The first compilation run resulted in a large number of diagnostic messages attributable to two principal errors: (a) accidental omission of the DATA DIVISION header, which prevented the File Section entries from being recognized and processed properly, and (b) failure to organize the entire Procedure Division into sections. (Originally, there were only sections at the end of the Procedure Division.) Upon correction of these errors, the program was resubmitted. This run compiled without errors and began to execute, but it was canceled by the operator due to an unexpected request for an output tape. This malfunction was quickly diagnosed, using an error code reference which revealed the necessity to provide a control card assigning a device for SORT-FILE in addition to those that had been provided for OUTPUT-FILE, CARD-FILE, and PRINT-FILE. Once this was accomplished, the run was resubmitted, and the desired outputs were obtained.

Exercise

1. Develop, in term paper form, a report summarizing your own experiences in learning COBOL. To what extent is the compiler which you use at fault? Can you cite examples of ambiguous, faulty, or missing diagnostic capability? What are the disadvantages of COBOL? Where should more emphasis be placed by the textbook and/or instructor? Is there a rational explanation for every trouble you have had in using COBOL?

   In developing this report, actual copies of computer runs are invaluable as a factual record of alleged mishaps.

10

SORT FEATURE

One of the most fundamental and frequently required business data processing techniques is file sorting, for often data is collected or produced in one order but required to be processed or reported in a different order. Accordingly, most COBOL compilers have implemented the file-sort feature, which is explained herein. The COBOL SORT feature necessitates a sort-file-definition in the File Section and a SORT statement in the Procedure Division. If required, two special statements may also be used to build a file to be sorted or to retrieve ordered records at the final stage of sorting. Appendix E contains a sample COBOL program containing a SORT statement. In fact, this program was used to produce the reserved word list in Appendix A.

10.1 General Description

Convenient use of the SORT subsystem can be made through a COBOL program. Interacting with the SORT subsystem, a COBOL object program may modify, insert, delete or summarize records during the initial or final phases of the sorting operation.

To use the SORT feature, the programmer provides sort-file definitions (having the special level indicator SD). There must be a SELECT sentence in the Environment Division for any SD-file. In an SD-entry, only the RECORD CONTAINS and DATA RECORDS clauses may appear. In the Procedure Division, the executable SORT statement initiates a sorting operation.

The format of this statement is:

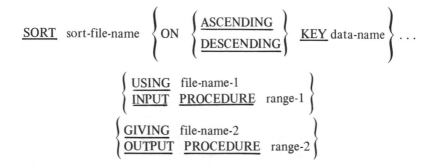

where ranges are defined as section-name-1 [THRU section-name-2]. The following discussions define the syntactic components of the SORT statement.

10.2 Ascending and Descending Keys

ASCENDING and DESCENDING specify whether the records are to be sorted into an ascending or descending sequence based on one or more sort keys. The sequence specified is applicable to all sort keys immediately following the keyword ASCENDING or DESCENDING. Both ASCENDING and DESCENDING may be specified in the same statement for different keys. Example:

SORT SFILE ASCENDING DEPARTMENT, DESCENDING RATE. . .

Sort keys must have a fixed length and may not be governed by an OCCURS clause (which would necessitate subscripting). The appropriate collating sequence, depending on key type, is used for each key. Sort keys are those data-names contained in the KEY clause of the SORT statement; all such names must be defined in record(s) subordinate to the sort-file-name. The major sort key is the first one in the KEY clause. Up to twelve sort keys may be defined per SORT. Every record which is listed in the DATA RECORDS clause of the sort-file must contain within its Record Description the KEY items data-name-1, data-name-2, etc.; each of the KEY items must have the same relative position in every one of the records. No two sort keys should overlap. A particular data item may be used once only in the KEY description.

10.3 SORT USING File-name-1

USING indicates that the records to be sorted are those of file-name-1 and that they are all to be passed to the sorting operation as one input file. If the programmer specifies the USING option, all the records to be sorted must be in the same file. This file will be automatically opened, read, and closed; the programmer must not attempt to do so himself. File-name-1 is defined by an **FD** entry, not a sort-file-definition.

10.4 SORT INPUT PROCEDURE

INPUT PROCEDURE indicates that the programmer has written an input procedure to process records before sorting and has included the procedure in the Procedure Division in the form of one or more distinct sections. The input procedure passes records one at a time to the SORT feature after it has completed its processing. In other words, the file to be sorted is built up by procedural statements in the specified range. The input procedure can include any statements needed to select, create, or modify records. Control must not be passed to the input procedure except by a SORT statement, because RELEASE statements (see below) have no meaning unless they are controlled by a SORT statement. The input procedure must not contain any SORT statements and must be fully "self-contained," in the sense that execution is not passed outside the range except to revert to the SORT subsystem. The input procedure must incorporate three specific functions:

1. It must build the records that are to be sorted, one at a time, in the data record that has been described for the sort-file. This can be accomplished by using statements such as READ...INTO...or MOVE. If the input is to come initially from a file, the program must open that file prior to executing the SORT statement.
2. Once a record has been built, the input procedure must make that record available to the sorting operation by means of the RELEASE statement, after which the record just built is no longer available. Either step 1 or step 3 is next.
3. When all the records have been released, control must pass to the last statement in the procedure in order to terminate the procedure. The EXIT statement provides a means of achieving this return to the SORT subsystem.

10.5 RELEASE Statement

The RELEASE statement, which can only appear in an input procedure, causes one record to be transferred to the sorting operation. If an input procedure is specified, the RELEASE statement must be included in that procedure. The format of the RELEASE statement is:

<u>RELEASE</u> record-name

where record-name is one of the data records in a sort-file-definition.

10.6 Sort GIVING file-name-2

GIVING indicates that, after the records have been sorted, they are to be written as a file on file-name-2. If the programmer specifies the GIVING option all records that have been sorted will be placed on one file. This file will be automatically opened, written, and closed by the SORT feature; the programmer must not attempt to do so himself. File-name-2 is defined by an FD entry, not a sort-file definition.

10.7 Sort OUTPUT PROCEDURE

OUTPUT PROCEDURE indicates that the programmer has written an output procedure to process records after they have been sorted and has included the procedure in the Procedure Division in the form of one or more distinct sections. The output procedure returns the records one at a time from the SORT feature after they have been sorted. In this case, the specified range retrieves the records in the order implied by the sort keys. The output procedure may consist of any statements needed to select, modify, or copy records being returned (one at a time, in sorted order) from the sort-file. Control must not be passed to the output procedure except by a SORT statement, since RETURN statements are meaningless unless controlled by a SORT statement. The output procedure must not include any SORT statements and must be self-contained. The programmer must code the output procedure so that it incorporates three specific functions:

1. It must obtain sorted records, one at a time, by means of the RETURN statement. Once a record has been returned, the previously returned record is no longer available.
2. It performs suitable output operations on each record returned. In order to produce an output file, the output procedure must properly open, write, and close it.
3. When the SORT feature has returned all records and the output procedure attempts to execute another RETURN statement (as in step 1), the AT END clause of the RETURN statement is executed. The imperative statement in the AT END clause must ultimately pass control to the last statement of the output procedure in order to

terminate the entire SORT operation. The EXIT statement is the usual means of achieving this termination.

10.8   RETURN Statement

The RETURN statement causes individual records to be obtained from the sorting operation after all the records have been sorted, and it indicates what action is to be taken with regard to each. The format of the RETURN statement is:

RETURN   sort-file-name

AT END   imperative-statement . . .

Note that, as in the READ statement, data is obtained by referring to the file-name. Data processing (as required in 10.7, step 2) employs appropriate record, group, and elementary item names contained in the sort-file record definition.

APPENDICES

Appendix A.

ACCEPT	ACCESS	ACTUAL	ADD
ADDRESS	ADVANCING	AFTER	ALL
ALPHABETIC	ALTER	ALTERNATE	AND
ARE	AREA	AREAS	ASCENDING
ASSIGN	AT	AUTHOR	BEFORE
BEGINNING	BLANK	BLOCK	BY
CF	CH	CHANGED	CHARACTERS
CLOCK-UNITS	CLOSE	COBOL	CODE
COLUMN	COMMA	COMMON-STORAGE	COMPUTATIONAL
COMPUTATIONAL-1	COMPUTATIONAL-2	COMPUTATIONAL-3	COMPUTE
CONFIGURATION	CONTAINS	CONTROL	CONTROLS
COPY	CORRESPONDING	CURRENCY	DATA
DATE-COMPILED	DATE-WRITTEN	DE	DECIMAL-POINT
DECLARATIVES	DEPENDING	DESCENDING	DETAIL
DISPLAY	DIVIDE	DIVISION	DOWN
ELSE	END	ENDING	ENTER
ENVIRONMENT	EQUAL	ERROR	EVERY
EXAMINE	EXHIBIT	EXIT	FD
FILE	FILE-CONTROL	FILE-LIMIT	FILE-LIMITS
FILLER	FINAL	FIRST	FOOTING
FOR	FROM	GENERATE	GIVING
GO	GREATER	GROUP	HEADING
HIGH-VALUE	HIGH-VALUES	I-O	I-O-CONTROL
IDENTIFICATION	IF	IN	INCLUDE
INDEX	INDEXED	INDICATE	INITIATE
INPUT	INPUT-OUTPUT	INSTALLATION	INTO
INVALID	IS	JUSTIFIED	KEY
LABEL	LAST	LEADING	LEFT
LESS	LIBRARY	LIMIT	LIMITS
LINE	LINE-COUNTER	LINES	LOCK
LOW-VALUE	LOW-VALUES	MEMORY	MODE
MODULES	MOVE	MULTIPLE	MULTIPLY
NAMED	NEGATIVE	NEXT	NO
NOT	NOTE	NUMBER	NUMERIC
OBJECT-COMPUTER	OCCURS	OF	OFF
OH	OMITTED	ON	OPEN
OPTIONAL	OR	OUTPUT	OV
OVERFLOW	PAGE	PAGE-COUNTER	PERFORM
PF	PH	PICTURE	PLUS
POSITION	POSITIVE	PROCEDURE	PROCEED
PROCESSING	PROGRAM-ID	QUOTE	QUOTES
RANDOM	RD	READ	READY
RECORD	RECORDS	REDEFINES	REEL
RELEASE	REMARKS	RENAMES	RENAMING
REPLACING	REPORT	REPORTING	REPORTS
RERUN	RESERVE	RESET	RETURN
REVERSED	REWIND	RF	RH
RIGHT	ROUNDED	RUN	SAME
SD	SEARCH	SECTION	SECURITY
SEEK	SEGMENT-LIMIT	SELECT	SELECTED
SENTENCE	SEQUENTIAL	SET	SIGN
SIZE	SORT	SOURCE	SOURCE-COMPUTER
SPACE	SPACES	SPECIAL-NAMES	STANDARD
STATUS	STOP	SUBTRACT	SUM
SYNCHRONIZED	TALLY	TALLYING	TAPE
TERMINATE	THAN	THRU	TIMES
TO	TRACE	TYPE	UNIT
UNTIL	UP	UPON	USAGE
USE	USING	VALUE	VALUES
VARYING	WHEN	WITH	WORDS
WORKING-STORAGE	WRITE	ZERO	ZERO

Appendix B   Card Punch Representations of Characters

Chart B-1   Letters, digits, minus, and slash.

ZONE PUNCH

		None	12	11	0
	None	blank		–	0
	1	1	A	J	/
	2	2	B	K	S
	3	3	C	L	T
Digit Punch	4	4	D	M	U
	5	5	E	N	V
	6	6	F	O	W
	7	7	G	P	X
	8	8	H	Q	Y
	9	9	I	R	Z

Chart B-2   Special characters.

	System		
Character	EBCDIC	BCD	RCA 301
+	12-8-6	12	12-8-2
*	11-8-4	11-8-4	11-8-4
=	8-6	8-3	0-8-6
$	11-8-3	11-8-3	11-8-3
,	0-8-3	0-8-3	0-8-3
;	11-8-6		12-8-4
.	12-8-3	12-8-3	12-8-3
'	8-5	8-4	12-8-6
(	12-8-5	0-8-4	8-5
)	11-8-5	12-8-4	8-6
>	0-8-6	8-6	
<	12-8-4	12-8-6	

Notes

1. EBCDIC is the card character code in IBM System 360, RCA Spectra 70, and XDS Sigma computers.
2. BCD is the card character code in most 6-bit Character computers, e.g., Univac 1108, IBM 7094, etc. For contrast, we also include the RCA 301 code, which differs from both BCD and EBCDIC.

Appendix C

```
    1   000010 IDENTIFICATION DIVISION.                                      TAPEUPD
    2   000020 PROGRAM-ID. 'TAPEUPD'.                                        TAPEUPD
    3   000030 REMARKS.  OPTION 'ORIGINATE' CREATES PHASE MASTER TAPE,       TAPEUPD
    4   000040          OPTION 'UPDATE' ACCEPTS CARD CHANGES AND             TAPEUPD
    5   000050          MAKES UPDATED MASTER.                                TAPEUPD
    6   000070 ENVIRONMENT DIVISION.                                         TAPEUPD
    7   000080 INPUT-OUTPUT SECTION.                                         TAPEUPD
    8   000090 FILE-CONTROL.                                                 TAPEUPD
    9   000100     SELECT OLD-MASTER, ASSIGN TO 'SYS011' UTILITY 2400.       TAPEUPD
   10   000110     SELECT NEW-MASTER, ASSIGN TO 'SYS012' UTILITY 2400.       TAPEUPD
   11   000120     SELECT CARDS,      ASSIGN TO 'SYS006' UNIT-RECORD 2540R.  TAPEUPD
   12   000130     SELECT LISTING,    ASSIGN TO 'SYS008' UNIT-RECORD 1403.   TAPEUPD
   13   000140 DATA DIVISION.                                                TAPEUPD
   14   000150 FILE SECTION.                                                 TAPEUPD
   15   000160 FD  OLD-MASTER DATA RECORD OLD  RECORDING MODE F              TAPEUPD
   16   000170     RECORD CONTAINS 80 CHARACTERS  LABEL RECORDS OMITTED.     TAPEUPD
   17   000180 01  OLD.                                                      TAPEUPD
   18   000190     02 BASE-PART        PICTURE X(75).                        TAPEUPD
   19   000200     02 NUMERIC-PART     PICTURE 9(5).                         TAPEUPD
   20   000210 FD  CARDS  DATA RECORD CD   RECORDING MODE F                  TAPEUPD
   21   000220     RECORD CONTAINS 80 CHARACTERS  LABEL RECORDS OMITTED.     TAPEUPD
   22   000230 01  CD.                                                       TAPEUPD
   23   000240     02 DELETE  PICTURE X(6).                                  TAPEUPD
   24   000250     02 FILLER  PICTURE X(3).                                  TAPEUPD
   25   000260     02 RANGE1  PICTURE 9(5).                                  TAPEUPD
   26   000270     02 FILLER  PICTURE X.                                     TAPEUPD
   27   000280     02 RANGE2  PICTURE 9(5).                                  TAPEUPD
   28   000290     02 RANGER  REDEFINES RANGE2  PICTURE XXXXX.               TAPEUPD
   29   000300     02 FILLER  PICTURE X(60).                                 TAPEUPD
   30   000310 FD  LISTING DATA RECORD LS RECORDING MODE F                   TAPEUPD
   31   000320     RECORD CONTAINS 133 CHARACTERS LABEL RECORDS OMITTED.     TAPEUPD
   32   000330 01  LS.                                                       TAPEUPD
   33   000340     02 FILLER  PICTURE X.                                     TAPEUPD
   34   000350     02 LS-1    PICTURE X(132).                                TAPEUPD
   35   000360 FD  NEW-MASTER  DATA RECORD NEW  RECORDING MODE F             TAPEUPD
   36   000370     RECORD CONTAINS 80 CHARACTERS LABEL RECORDS OMITTED.      TAPEUPD
   37   000380 01  NEW.                                                      TAPEUPD
   38   000390     02 NEW-BASE          PICTURE X(75).                       TAPEUPD
   39   000400     02 NEW-NUMERIC       PICTURE 9(5).                        TAPEUPD
   40   000410                                                               TAPEUPD
   41   000420 WORKING-STORAGE SECTION.                                      TAPEUPD
   42   000430 01  CHOICE.                                                   TAPEUPD
   43   000440     02  ORIGINATE    PICTURE X(9).                            TAPEUPD
   44   000450     02  FILLER REDEFINES ORIGINATE.                           TAPEUPD
   45   000460         03 UP     PICTURE X(6).                               TAPEUPD
   46   000470         03 FILLER  PICTURE X(3).                              TAPEUPD
   47   000480     02  TRACER PICTURE X.                                     TAPEUPD
   48   000490 01  CD-EOF PICTURE X  VALUE SPACE.                            TAPEUPD
   49   000500 01  COUNTER  PICTURE 9(5), VALUE 1.                           TAPEUPD
   50   000510 01  CD-SAVE.                                                  TAPEUPD
   51   000520     02 ACTION     PICTURE X(6).                               TAPEUPD
   52   000530     02 FILLER     PICTURE X(3).                               TAPEUPD
   53   000540     02 R1         PICTURE 9(5), VALUE ZERO.                   TAPEUPD
   54   000550     02 FILLER     PICTURE X.                                  TAPEUPD
   55   000560     02 R2         PICTURE 9(5), VALUE 99999.                  TAPEUPD
   56   000570 01  SWITCH    PICTURE 9  VALUE 0.                             TAPEUPD
   57   000580 PROCEDURE DIVISION.                                           TAPEUPD
   58   000590     OPEN INPUT CARDS, OUTPUT              LISTING.            TAPEUPD
   59   000600     OPEN OUTPUT NEW-MASTER.                                   TAPEUPD
   60   000610     READ CARDS AT END GO TO BAD-CONTROL-CARD.                 TAPEUPD
   61   000620     MOVE CD TO CHOICE.                                        TAPEUPD
   62   000630     IF  TRACER NOT = SPACE  READY TRACE.                      TAPEUPD
   63   000640     IF ORIGINATE = 'ORIGINATE' GO TO ORIG.                    TAPEUPD
   64   000650     IF UP NOT = 'UPDATE'   *  GO TO BAD-CONTROL-CARD.         TAPEUPD
   65   000660     OPEN INPUT OLD-MASTER WITH NO REWIND.                     TAPEUPD
   66   000670     ALTER RCD TO PROCEED TO RIF.                              TAPEUPD
   67   000680 UPDATER.   PERFORM READ-CARD.                                 TAPEUPD
   68   000690 AGAIN.  PERFORM READ-OLD.                                     TAPEUPD
   69   000700 TEST.  IF NUMERIC-PART = R1 GO TO BRANCH-UPDATE.              TAPEUPD
   70   000710     PERFORM COPY-OLD  GO TO AGAIN.                            TAPEUPD
   71   000720                                                               TAPEUPD
   72   000730 BRANCH-UPDATE.  GO TO INS DRP OTH DEPENDING ON SWITCH.        TAPEUPD
```

117

```
 73    000740 OTH.  STOP '**** IMPOSSIBLE ***'.  STOP RUN.                 TAPEUPD
 74    000750 INS.  PERFORM COPY-OLD.                                      TAPEUPD
 75    000760                                                              TAPEUPD
 76    000770 COPY-FROM-CD.  PERFORM READ-CARD. IF SWITCH = 3              TAPEUPD
 77    000780        MOVE CD TO OLD PERFORM COPY-OLD GO TO COPY-FROM-CD.   TAPEUPD
 78    000790        IF CD-EOF NOT = SPACE GO TO FINISH-UPDATE.            TAPEUPD
 79    000800        GO TO AGAIN.                                          TAPEUPD
 80    000810                                                              TAPEUPD
 81    000820 DRP.  IF NUMERIC-PART NOT GREATER THAN R2                    TAPEUPD
 82    000830        PERFORM READ-OLD  GO TO DRP, ELSE                     TAPEUPD
 83    000840        PERFORM READ-CARD GO TO TEST.                         TAPEUPD
 84    000850                                                              TAPEUPD
 85    000860 READ-CARD SECTION.                                           TAPEUPD
 86    C00870        IF CD-EOF NOT = SPACE GO TO EMERGE.                   TAPEUPD
 87    000880        READ CARDS AT END GO TO BYPASS.                       TAPEUPD
 88    000890        MOVE CD TO LS-1  PERFORM LIST-OUT.                    TAPEUPD
 89    000900 RCD.  GO TO EMERGE.                                          TAPEUPD
 90    000910 RIF.                                                         TAPEUPD
 91    000920        IF DELETE = 'DELETE' GO TO CK-DELETE.                 TAPEUPD
 92    000930        IF DELETE = 'INSERT' MOVE 1 TO SWITCH  GO TO CK-INSERT, TAPEUPD
 93    000940        ELSE MOVE 3 TO SWITCH  GO TO EMERGE.                  TAPEUPD
 94    000950                                                              TAPEUPD
 95    000960 BYPASS.  MOVE ZERO TO R1   MOVE 99999 TO R2                  TAPEUPD
 96    000970        MOVE  4 TO SWITCH.                                    TAPEUPD
 97    000980        MOVE 'A' TO CD-EOF                                    TAPEUPD
 98    000990        GO TO EMERGE.                                         TAPEUPD
 99    001000                                                              TAPEUPD
100    001010 CK-DELETE.  MOVE 2 TO SWITCH.                                TAPEUPD
101    001020        IF RANGER = SPACES MOVE RANGE1 TO RANGE2, GO TO CK-INSERT. TAPEUPD
102    001030        IF RANGE2 NOT NUMERIC                                 TAPEUPD
103    001040        MOVE ' SECOND NUMBER OF RANGE NOT NUMERIC.' TO        TAPEUPD
104    001050        LS-1 PERFORM LIST-OUT  CLOSE LISTING STOP RUN.        TAPEUPD
105    001060        IF RANGE1 GREATER THAN RANGE2 MOVE 'BAD SECOND RANGE * * *' TAPEUPD
106    001070        TO LS-1  PERFORM LIST-OUT  GO TO OTH.                 TAPEUPD
107    001080                                                              TAPEUPD
108    001090 CK-INSERT.                                                   TAPEUPD
109    001100        IF RANGE1 NOT NUMERIC                                 TAPEUPD
110    001110        MOVE ' RANGE NOT NUMERIC.'                            TAPEUPD
111    001120        TO LS-1  PERFORM LIST-OUT CLOSE LISTING STOP RUN.     TAPEUPD
112    001130        IF RANGE1 NOT > R1  MOVE 'ILLEGAL ORDER OF CHANGES * * *' TAPEUPD
113    001140        TO LS-1  PERFORM LIST-OUT   GO TO OTH.                TAPEUPD
114    001150        MOVE CD TO CD-SAVE.                                   TAPEUPD
115    001160 EMERGE.  EXIT.                                               TAPEUPD
116    001170                                                              TAPEUPD
117    001180 LIST-OUT SECTION.                                           TAPEUPD
118    001190        WRITE LS  AFTER ADVANCING  1 LINES.                   TAPEUPD
119    001200                                                              TAPEUPD
120    001210 READ-OLD SECTION.                                            TAPEUPD
121    001220        READ OLD-MASTER AT END GO TO EOFF.                    TAPEUPD
122    001230                                                              TAPEUPD
123    001240 COPY-OLD SECTION.                                            TAFCUPD
124    001250        MOVE OLD TO NEW  MOVE COUNTER TO NEW-NUMERIC          TAPEUPD
125    001260        WRITE NEW ADD 1 TO COUNTER.                           TAPEUPD
126    001270                                                              TAPEUPD
127    001280 ORIG SECTION.                                                TAPEUPD
128    001290        PERFORM READ-CARD.                                    TAPEUPD
129    001300        IF CD-EOF = SPACE GO TO DUPLICATE ELSE CLOSE LISTING, CARDS. TAPEUPD
130    001310        EXHIBIT NAMED COUNTER.                                TAPEUPD
131    001320        CLOSE NEW-MASTER                      STOP RUN.       TAPEUPD
132    001330 DUPLICATE.                                                   TAPEUPD
133    001340        MOVE CD TO NEW  MOVE COUNTER TO NEW-NUMERIC           TAPEUPD
134    001350        WRITE NEW  ADD 1 TO COUNTER   GO TO ORIG.             TAPEUPD
135    001360                                                              TAPEUPD
136    001370 FINISH-UPDATE SECTION.                                       TAPEUPD
137    001380        PERFORM READ-OLD THRU COPY-OLD  9999 TIMES.           TAPEUPD
138    001390        DISPLAY 'RUN-AWAY IN UPDATING AFTER LAST CHANGE.'  STOP RUN. TAPEUPD
139    001400                                                              TAPEUPD
140    001410 BAD-CONTROL-CARD  SECTION.                                   TAPEUPD
141    001420        MOVE 'OPTION CARD FAILURE * * *'  TO  LS-1  PERFORM LIST-OUT. TAPEUPD
142    001430        CLOSE LISTING  CARDS  STOP RUN.                       TAPEUPD
143    001440 EOFF SECTION.                                                TAPEUPD
144    001450        CLOSE  NEW-MASTER OLD-MASTER LISTING.                 TAPEUPD
145    001460        EXHIBIT NAMED COUNTER.                                TAPEUPD
146    001470        DISPLAY 'END-OF-JOB' UPON CONSOLE STOP RUN.           TAPEUPD
```

Appendix D   RESEQ Program Listing

RESEQ is used in resequencing source-language decks. It may be applied to *either* assembly-language decks or COBOL decks by suitable specifications in a special control card:

Field (Card Columns)	Content and Meaning
1	Must contain quote (5-8 punch)
2-9	New-id (left justified)
10	Quote (not mandatory)
12-13	Location of new-sequence number
15-22	Initial value (8 digits)
24-29	Increment (6 digits)

Interpretation of the Fields in the Control Card. For COBOL, output decks are resequenced in columns 1 through 6. Therefore, "Location of new sequence number" is left blank (or contains 00). In this case, the new-id is automatically placed in columns 73-80. For assembly-language source decks, or any deck to be re-identified and re-sequenced in columns 73-80, the number in card columns 12-13 of the control card may be from 73 to 80, signifying the position in the output card in which the new sequence numbers will appear. The first sequence number is as supplied in control card columns 15-22; successive numbers are formed by the addition of the increment given in control card columns 24-29. The new-id appears in those output columns to the left of "location of new-sequence number." A copy of the punched cards is listed on the 1403 printer.

```
   1   000010 IDENTIFICATION DIVISION.                                        RESEQ
   2   000020 PROGRAM-ID.                                                     RESEQ
   3   000030     'RESEQ'.                                                    RESEQ
   4   000080 REMARKS.  RESEQUENCES EITHER AN ASSEMBLY LANGUAGE OR            RESEQ
   5   000090          COBOL PROGRAM, THE LATTER IN COLUMNS 1 THRU 6          RESEQ
   6   000100          AND THE FORMER IN COLUMNS 73 THRU 80.                  RESEQ
   7   000110 ENVIRONMENT DIVISION.                                           RESEQ
   8   000120 CONFIGURATION SECTION.                                          RESEQ
   9   000130 SOURCE-COMPUTER.        IBM-360.                                RESEQ
  10   000140 OBJECT-COMPUTER.        IBM-360.                                RESEQ
  11   000150 INPUT-OUTPUT SECTION.                                           RESEQ
  12   000160 FILE-CONTROL.                                                   RESEQ
  13   000170     SELECT IN-FILE ASSIGN TO 'SYS011' UNIT-RECORD 2540P.        RESEQ
  14   000180     SELECT PUNCH-FILE ASSIGN TO 'SYS013' UNIT-RECORD 2540P.     RESEQ
  15   000190     SELECT PRINT-FILE ASSIGN TO 'SYS015' UNIT-RECORD 1403.      RESEQ
  16   000200 DATA DIVISION.                                                  RESEQ
  17   000210 FILE SECTION.                                                   RESEQ
  18   000220 FD  IN-FILE            RECORDING MODE IS F                      RESEQ
  19   000230                        RECORD CONTAINS 80 CHARACTERS            RESEQ
  20   000240                        LABEL RECORD IS OMITTED                  RESEQ
  21   000250                        DATA RECORD IS IN-REC.                   RESEQ
  22   000260 01  IN-REC             PICTURE X(80).                           RESEQ
  23   000270 FD  PUNCH-FILE         RECORDING MODE IS F                      RESEQ
  24   000280                        RECORD CONTAINS 80 CHARACTERS            RESEQ
  25   000290                        LABEL RECORD IS OMITTED                  RESEQ
  26   000300                        DATA RECORD IS OUTPUT-RECORD.            RESEQ
  27   000310 01  OUTPUT-RECORD      PICTURE X(80).                           RESEQ
  28   000320 FD  PRINT-FILE         RECORDING MODE IS F                      RESEQ
  29   000330                        RECORD CONTAINS 133 CHARACTERS           RESEQ
  30   000340                        LABEL RECORD IS OMITTED                  RESEQ
  31   000350                        DATA RECORD IS PRINT-RECORD.             RESEQ
  32   000360 01  PRINT-RECORD.                                               RESEQ
  33   000370     05  CTL      PICTURE X.                                     RESEQ
  34   000380     05  OUT-LINE PICTURE X(132).                               RESEQ
  35   000390 WORKING-STORAGE SECTION.                                        RESEQ
  36   000560 77  LINE-COUNT   PICTURE S999 VALUE 100  COMPUTATIONAL-3.       RESEQ
  37   000570 77  LOC          PICTURE S9.                                    RESEQ
  38   000400 01  NEW-VALUE    PICTURE 9(8).                                  RESEQ
  39   000410 01  FILLER  REDEFINES NEW-VALUE.                                RESEQ
  40   000420     02 FILLER   PICTURE X.                                      RESEQ
  41   000430     02 VAL-74.                                                  RESEQ
  42   000440       03 FILLER PICTURE X.                                      RESEQ
  43   000450       03 VAL-75.                                                RESEQ
  44   000460         04 FILLER   PICTURE X.                                  RESEQ
  45   000470         04 VAL-76.                                              RESEQ
  46   000480           05 FILLER PICTURE X.                                  RESEQ
  47   000490           05 VAL-77.                                            RESEQ
  48   000500             06 FILLER   PICTURE X.                              RESEQ
  49   000510             06 VAL-78.                                          RESEQ
  50   000520               07 FILLER PICTURE X.                             RESEQ
  51   000530               07 VAL-79.                                        RESEQ
  52   000540                 08 FILLER   PICTURE X.                          RESEQ
  53   000550                 08 VAL-80  PICTURE X.                           RESEQ
  54   000580 01  CARD1-IN.                                                   RESEQ
  55   000590     02 PART1      PICTURE X(72).                                RESEQ
  56   000600     02 PART2      PICTURE X(8).                                 RESEQ
  57   000610 01  CARD2-IN REDEFINES CARD1-IN.                                RESEQ
  58   000620     02 SECT1      PICTURE X(6).                                 RESEQ
  59   000630     02 SECT2      PICTURE X(66).                                RESEQ
  60   000640     02 SECT3      PICTURE X(8).                                 RESEQ
  61   000650 01  OUT-REC.                                                    RESEQ
  62   000660     02 LOCATION-1  PICTURE X(72).                               RESEQ
  63   000670     02 LOCATION-2  PICTURE X(8).                                RESEQ
  64   000680     02 DUMMY-LOC   REDEFINES       LOCATION-2.                  RESEQ
  65   000690       03 COLUMN-73.                                             RESEQ
  66   000700         04 FILLER                          PICTURE X.           RESEQ
  67   000710         04 COLUMN-74.                                           RESEQ
  68   000720           05 FILLER                        PICTURE X.           RESEQ
  69   000730           05 COLUMN-75.                                         RESEQ
  70   000740             06 FILLER                      PICTURE X.           RESEQ
  71   000750             06 COLUMN-76.                                       RESEQ
  72   000760               07 FILLER                    PICTURE X.           RESEQ
  73   000770               07 COLUMN-77.                                     RESEQ
  74   000780                 08 FILLER                  PICTURE X.           RESEQ
  75   000790                 08 COLUMN-78.                                   RESEQ
  76   000800                   09 FILLER      PICTURE X.                     RESEQ
  77   000810                   09 COLUMN-79.                                 RESEQ
  78   000820                     10 FILLER PICTURE X.                        RESEQ
  79   000830                     10 COLUMN-80  PICTURE X.                    RESEQ
  80   000840 01  OUTPUT-REC.                                                 RESEQ
  81   000850     05  LOCASION-1  PICTURE S9(6).                              RESEQ
  82   000860     02  LOCASION-2  PICTURE X(66).                              RESEQ
  83   000870     02  LOCASION-3  PICTURE X(8).                               RESEQ
```

```
 84    000880 01  CONTROL-CARD.                                            RESEQ
 85    000890     02 CHAR-1               PICTURE  X.                      RESEQ
 86    000900     02 NEW-ID               PICTURE  X(8).                   RESEQ
 87    000910     02 CHAR-2               PICTURE  X.                      RESEQ
 88    000920     02 FILLER               PICTURE  X.                      RESEQ
 89    000930     02 NEW-ID-LOC           PICTURE  S99.                    RESEQ
 90    000940     02 FILLER               PICTURE  X.                      RESEQ
 91    000950     02 INITIAL-VALUE        PICTURE  S9(8).                  RESEQ
 92    000960     02 FILLER               PICTURE  X.                      RESEQ
 93    000970     02 INCREMENT            PICTURE  S9(6).                  RESEQ
 94    000980 PROCEDURE DIVISION.                                         RESEQ
 95    000990 START-PROCESSING.                                          RESEQ
 96    001000     OPEN INPUT IN-FILE                                     RESEQ
 97    001010         OUTPUT PUNCH-FILE, PRINT-FILE.                     RESEQ
 98    001020 READ-AND-CHECK-RECORD.                                     RESEQ
 99    001030     READ IN-FILE INTO CONTROL-CARD  AT END GO TO END-OF-RUN. RESEQ
100    001040     IF INCREMENT NOT NUMERIC OR INITIAL-VALUE NOT NUMERIC  RESEQ
101    001050         OR CHAR-1 NOT EQUAL TO QUOTE, DISPLAY              RESEQ
102    001060         'BAD CONTROL CARD', GO TO END-OF-RUN.             RESEQ
103    001070 DATA-CARD-READ.                                            RESEQ
104    001080     READ IN-FILE INTO CARD1-IN AT END GO TO END-OF-RUN.   RESEQ
105    001090     IF NEW-ID-LOC NOT NUMERIC OR NEW-ID-LOC ZERO          RESEQ
106    001100         GO TO COBOL-RESEQ.                                RESEQ
107    001110     MOVE PART1 TO LOCATION-1 OF OUT-REC.                  RESEQ
108    001120     MOVE NEW-ID TO LOCATION-2.                            RESEQ
109    001130     ADD INCREMENT, INITIAL-VALUE, GIVING NEW-VALUE.       RESEQ
110    001140     SUBTRACT 72 FROM NEW-ID-LOC GIVING LOC.               RESEQ
111    001150     GO TO LOC73, LOC74, LOC75, LOC76,                     RESEQ
112    001160         LOC77, LOC78, LOC79, LOC80        DEPENDING ON LOC. RESEQ
113    001170     DISPLAY 'IMPROPER NEW-ID-LOC' GO TO END-OF-RUN.       RESEQ
114    001180 LOC73.                                                     RESEQ
115    001190     MOVE NEW-VALUE TO COLUMN-73 OF OUT-REC.               RESEQ
116    001200     GO TO   WRITE-REC.                                    RESEQ
117    001210 LOC74.                                                     RESEQ
118    001220     MOVE  VAL-74   TO COLUMN-74 OF OUT-REC.               RESEQ
119    001230     GO TO   WRITE-REC.                                    RESEQ
120    001240 LOC75.                                                     RESEQ
121    001250     MOVE  VAL-75   TO COLUMN-75 OF OUT-REC.               RESEQ
122    001260     GO TO   WRITE-REC.                                    RESEQ
123    001270 LOC76.                                                     RESEQ
124    001280     MOVE  VAL-76   TO COLUMN-76 OF OUT-REC.               RESEQ
125    001290     GO TO   WRITE-REC.                                    RESEQ
126    001300 LOC77.                                                     RESEQ
127    001310     MOVE  VAL-77   TO COLUMN-77 OF OUT-REC.               RESEQ
128    001320     GO TO   WRITE-REC.                                    RESEQ
129    001330 LOC78.                                                     RESEQ
130    001340     MOVE  VAL-78   TO COLUMN-78 OF OUT-REC.               RESEQ
131    001350     GO TO   WRITE-REC.                                    RESEQ
132    001360 LOC79.                                                     RESEQ
133    001370     MOVE  VAL-79   TO COLUMN-79 OF OUT-REC.               RESEQ
134    001380     GO TO   WRITE-REC.                                    RESEQ
135    001390 LOC80.                                                     RESEQ
136    001400     MOVE  VAL-80   TO COLUMN-80 OF OUT-REC.               RESEQ
137    001410     GO TO   WRITE-REC.                                    RESEQ
138    001420 WRITE-REC.                                                 RESEQ
139    001430     WRITE OUTPUT-RECORD FROM OUT-REC.                     RESEQ
140    001440     IF LINE-COUNT GREATER THAN 50                         RESEQ
141    001450         MOVE SPACES TO PRINT-RECORD                       RESEQ
142    001460         WRITE PRINT-RECORD AFTER 0                        RESEQ
143    001470         MOVE 0 TO LINE-COUNT.                             RESEQ
144    001480     MOVE OUT-REC TO OUT-LINE.                             RESEQ
145    001490     WRITE PRINT-RECORD AFTER 1.                           RESEQ
146    001500     ADD 1 TO LINE-COUNT.                                  RESEQ
147    001510     MOVE NEW-VALUE TO INITIAL-VALUE.                      RESEQ
148    001520     GO TO DATA-CARD-READ.                                 RESEQ
149    001530 COBOL-RESEQ.                                               RESEQ
150    001540     ADD INCREMENT, INITIAL-VALUE, GIVING NEW-VALUE.       RESEQ
151    001550     MOVE SECT2 TO LOCASION-2 OF OUTPUT-REC.               RESEQ
152    001560     MOVE NEW-VALUE TO LOCASION-1 OF OUTPUT-REC.           RESEQ
153    001570     MOVE NEW-ID TO LOCATION-3 OF OUTPUT-REC.              RESEQ
154    001580     WRITE OUTPUT-RECORD FROM OUTPUT-REC.                  RESEQ
155    001590     IF LINE-COUNT GREATER THAN 50                         RESEQ
156    001600         MOVE SPACES TO PRINT-RECORD                       RESEQ
157    001610         WRITE PRINT-RECORD AFTER 0                        RESEQ
158    001620         MOVE 0 TO LINE-COUNT.                             RESEQ
159    001630     MOVE OUTPUT-REC TO OUT-LINE.                          RESEQ
160    001640     WRITE PRINT-RECORD AFTER 1.                           RESEQ
161    001650     ADD 1 TO LINE-COUNT.                                  RESEQ
162    001660     MOVE NEW-VALUE TO INITIAL-VALUE.                      RESEQ
163    001670     GO TO DATA-CARD-READ.                                 RESEQ
164    001680 END-OF-RUN.                                                RESEQ
165    001690     CLOSE IN-FILE, PUNCH-FILE, PRINT-FILE.                RESEQ
166    001700     STOP RUN.                                             RESEQ
```

Appendix E

```
COO          COBOL SOURCE PROGRAM AND DIAGNOSTIC LISTING

00000          COBOL LS,XREF,GO
00001              IDENTIFICATION DIVISION.
00002              PROGRAM-ID.  RWLIST.
00003              ENVIRONMENT DIVISION.
00004              CONFIGURATION SECTION.
00005              SOURCE-COMPUTER.  XDS-SIGMA-7.
00006              OBJECT-COMPUTER.  XDS-SIGMA-7.
00007              SPECIAL-NAMES.  '1' IS TOP.
00008              INPUT-OUTPUT SECTION.
00009              FILE-CONTROL.
00010                  SELECT OUTPUT-FILE ASSIGN TO DISC.
00011                  SELECT PRINT-FILE ASSIGN TO PRINTER.
00012                  SELECT CARD-FILE ASSIGN TO CARD-READER.
00013                  SELECT SORT-FILE.
00014              DATA DIVISION.
00015              FILE SECTION.
00016              SD  SORT-FILE DATA RECORD IS S.
00017              01  S PICTURE X(30).
00018              FD  OUTPUT-FILE DATA RECORD IS D LABEL RECORDS STANDARD.
00019              01  D PICTURE X(30).
00020              FD  PRINT-FILE DATA RECORD IS P LABEL RECORDS OMITTED.
00021              01  P.
00022                  02 FILLER PICTURE X.
00023                  02 W OCCURS 4 PICTURE X(30).
00024              FD  CARD-FILE DATA RECORD C LABEL RECORDS OMITTED.
00025              01  C PICTURE X(80).
00026              WORKING-STORAGE SECTION.
00027              77  I COMPUTATIONAL.
00028              77  SWTCH PICTURE X VALUE SPACE.
00029              PROCEDURE DIVISION.
00030              MAIN-PROGRAM SECTION.
00031              STARTING-PARAGRAPH.
00032                  OPEN INPUT CARD-FILE  OUTPUT OUTPUT-FILE PRINT-FILE.
00033              READ-WORD-CARD.
00034                  READ CARD-FILE  AT END GO TO SORTING.
00035                  WRITE D FROM C  GO TO READ-WORD-CARD.
00036              SORTING.
00037                  MOVE ZERO TO TALLY.
00038                  CLOSE CARD-FILE  OUTPUT-FILE.
00039                  SORT SORT-FILE  ASCENDING KEY S USING OUTPUT-FILE
00040                      OUTPUT PROCEDURE WRITER.
00041                  CLOSE PRINT-FILE  STOP RUN.
00042              WRITER SECTION.
00043              GET-REC.
00044                  IF SWTCH = SPACE MOVE 'X' TO SWTCH MOVE SPACES TO P
00045                      WRITE P BEFORE ADVANCING TOP.
00046                  RETURN SORT-FILE RECORD  AT END GO TO END-WRITER.
00047                  ADD 1 TO TALLY.
00048                  IF TALLY GREATER THAN 4 WRITE P AFTER ADVANCING 1 LINE
00049                      MOVE 1 TO TALLY.  MOVE S TO W (TALLY).
00050                  GO  TO GET-REC.
00051              END-WRITER.
00052                  PERFORM BLANK-OUT VARYING I FROM TALLY BY 1 UNTIL I NOT
00053                      LESS THAN 5.  WRITE P.
00054              BLANK-OUT SECTION.
00055              B.  MOVE SPACES TO W (TALLY).

** NUMBER OF DIAGNOSTIC MESSAGES      0
```

COBOL

by Kenneth P. Seidel

From Kenneth Seidel's vast experience in the field of COBOL comes an introductory text that, in addition to offering simplified language rules and regulations, includes the insight and cautionary advice that only such a COBOL expert can provide.

FEATURES
Emphasizes IBM System 360 and other third-generation systems.

Devotes a complete chapter to a case study of a file maintenance program. An entire problem, from specification to flow chart, is presented. Includes three complete program listings as appendices, giving the reader a set of *realistic* examples promoting good technique as well as illustrating coding rules.

Includes another chapter devoted entirely to debugging.

Offers many illustrations and problems.

CHAPTER HEADINGS
What Is COBOL? COBOL Program Fundamentals. Data Files. COBOL File Descriptions. The Working-storage Section. The Procedure Division. Writing a COBOL File Maintenance Program. Advanced Topics. Debugging COBOL Programs. SORT Feature. Appendices.

KENNETH P. SEIDEL entered the computing field in 1957, working extensively with IBM for several years. He now maintains his own consulting enterprise, Seidel Computer Associates, and teaches computer science at the School of Business at San Fernando Valley State College.

GOODYEAR PUBLISHING CO., INC. ⊖
Pacific Palisades, California

0-87620-185-0